LAYERS OF LEARNING
YEAR FOUR • UNIT FIFTEEN

COLD WAR
U.S. TERRITORIES
CHEMISTRY OF MEDICINE
FREE VERSE

Published by HooDoo Publishing
United States of America
© 2017 Layers of Learning
Copies of maps or activities may be made for a particular family or classroom. All other rights reserved. Printed in the United States of America.
(Grilled Cheese BTN Font) © Fontdiner - www.fontdiner.com
ISBN #978-1548764685

Units at a Glance: Topics For All Four Years of the Layers of Learning Program

1	History	Geography	Science	The Arts
1	Mesopotamia	Maps & Globes	Planets	Cave Paintings
2	Egypt	Map Keys	Stars	Egyptian Art
3	Europe	Global Grids	Earth & Moon	Crafts
4	Ancient Greece	Wonders	Satellites	Greek Art
5	Babylon	Mapping People	Humans in Space	Poetry
6	The Levant	Physical Earth	Laws of Motion	List Poems
7	Phoenicians	Oceans	Motion	Moral Stories
8	Assyrians	Deserts	Fluids	Rhythm
9	Persians	Arctic	Waves	Melody
10	Ancient China	Forests	Machines	Chinese Art
11	Early Japan	Mountains	States of Matter	Line & Shape
12	Arabia	Rivers & Lakes	Atoms	Color & Value
13	Ancient India	Grasslands	Elements	Texture & Form
14	Ancient Africa	Africa	Bonding	African Tales
15	First North Americans	North America	Salts	Creative Kids
16	Ancient South America	South America	Plants	South American Art
17	Celts	Europe	Flowering Plants	Jewelry
18	Roman Republic	Asia	Trees	Roman Art
19	Christianity	Australia & Oceania	Simple Plants	Instruments
20	Roman Empire	You Explore	Fungi	Composing Music

2	History	Geography	Science	The Arts
1	Byzantines	Turkey	Climate & Seasons	Byzantine Art
2	Barbarians	Ireland	Forecasting	Illumination
3	Islam	Arabian Peninsula	Clouds & Precipitation	Creative Kids
4	Vikings	Norway	Special Effects	Viking Art
5	Anglo Saxons	Britain	Wild Weather	King Arthur Tales
6	Charlemagne	France	Cells & DNA	Carolingian Art
7	Normans	Nigeria	Skeletons	Canterbury Tales
8	Feudal System	Germany	Muscles, Skin, Cardio	Gothic Art
9	Crusades	Balkans	Digestive & Senses	Religious Art
10	Burgundy, Venice, Spain	Switzerland	Nerves	Oil Paints
11	Wars of the Roses	Russia	Health	Minstrels & Plays
12	Eastern Europe	Hungary	Metals	Printmaking
13	African Kingdoms	Mali	Carbon Chemistry	Textiles
14	Asian Kingdoms	Southeast Asia	Non-metals	Vivid Language
15	Mongols	Caucasus	Gases	Fun With Poetry
16	Medieval China & Japan	China	Electricity	Asian Arts
17	Pacific Peoples	Micronesia	Circuits	Arts of the Islands
18	American Peoples	Canada	Technology	Indian Legends
19	The Renaissance	Italy	Magnetism	Renaissance Art I
20	Explorers	Caribbean Sea	Motors	Renaissance Art II

www.Layers-of-Learning.com

3	History	Geography	Science	The Arts
1	Age of Exploration	Argentina & Chile	Classification & Insects	Fairy Tales
2	The Ottoman Empire	Egypt & Libya	Reptiles & Amphibians	Poetry
3	Mogul Empire	Pakistan & Afghanistan	Fish	Mogul Arts
4	Reformation	Angola & Zambia	Birds	Reformation Art
5	Renaissance England	Tanzania & Kenya	Mammals & Primates	Shakespeare
6	Thirty Years' War	Spain	Sound	Baroque Music
7	The Dutch	Netherlands	Light & Optics	Baroque Art I
8	France	Indonesia	Bending Light	Baroque Art II
9	The Enlightenment	Korean Peninsula	Color	Art Journaling
10	Russia & Prussia	Central Asia	History of Science	Watercolors
11	Conquistadors	Baltic States	Igneous Rocks	Creative Kids
12	Settlers	Peru & Bolivia	Sedimentary Rocks	Native American Art
13	13 Colonies	Central America	Metamorphic Rocks	Settler Sayings
14	Slave Trade	Brazil	Gems & Minerals	Colonial Art
15	The South Pacific	Australasia	Fossils	Principles of Art
16	The British in India	India	Chemical Reactions	Classical Music
17	The Boston Tea Party	Japan	Reversible Reactions	Folk Music
18	Founding Fathers	Iran	Compounds & Solutions	Rococo
19	Declaring Independence	Samoa & Tonga	Oxidation & Reduction	Creative Crafts I
20	The American Revolution	South Africa	Acids & Bases	Creative Crafts II

4	History	Geography	Science	The Arts
1	American Government	USA	Heat & Temperature	Patriotic Music
2	Expanding Nation	Pacific States	Motors & Engines	Tall Tales
3	Industrial Revolution	U.S. Landscapes	Energy	Romantic Art I
4	Revolutions	Mountain West States	Energy Sources	Romantic Art II
5	Africa	U.S. Political Maps	Energy Conversion	Impressionism I
6	The West	Southwest States	Earth Structure	Impressionism II
7	Civil War	National Parks	Plate Tectonics	Post Impressionism
8	World War I	Plains States	Earthquakes	Expressionism
9	Totalitarianism	U.S. Economics	Volcanoes	Abstract Art
10	Great Depression	Heartland States	Mountain Building	Kinds of Art
11	World War II	Symbols & Landmarks	Chemistry of Air & Water	War Art
12	Modern East Asia	The South	Food Chemistry	Modern Art
13	India's Independence	People of America	Industry	Pop Art
14	Israel	Appalachian States	Chemistry of Farming	Modern Music
15	Cold War	U.S. Territories	Chemistry of Medicine	Free Verse
16	Vietnam War	Atlantic States	Food Chains	Photography
17	Latin America	New England States	Animal Groups	Latin American Art
18	Civil Rights	Home State Study I	Instincts	Theater & Film
19	Technology	Home State Study II	Habitats	Architecture
20	Terrorism	America in Review	Conservation	Creative Kids

Unit 4-15

Printable Pack

This unit includes printables at the end. To make life easier for you we also created digital printable packs for each unit. To retrieve your printable pack for Unit 4-15, please visit

www.layers-of-learning.com/digital-printable-packs/

Put the printable pack in your shopping cart and use this coupon code:

627UNIT4-15

Your printable pack will be free.

Layers of Learning Introduction

This is part of a series of units in the Layers of Learning homeschool curriculum, including the subjects of history, geography, science, and the arts. Children from 1st through 12th can participate in the same curriculum at the same time - family school style.

The units are intended to be used in order as the basis of a complete curriculum (once you add in a systematic math, reading, and writing program). You begin with Year 1 Unit 1 no matter what ages your children are. Spend about 2 weeks on each unit. You pick and choose the activities within the unit that appeal to you and read the books from the book list that are available to you or find others on the same topic from your library. We highly recommend that you use the timeline in every history section as the backbone. Then flesh out your learning with reading and activities that highlight the topics you think are the most important.

Alternatively, you can use the units as activity ideas to supplement another curriculum in any order you wish. You can still use them with all ages of children at the same time.

When you've finished with Year One, move on to Year Two, Year Three, and Year Four. Then begin again with Year One and work your way through the years again. Now your children will be older, reading more involved books, and writing more in depth. When you have completed the sequence for the second time, you start again on it for the third and final time. If your student began with Layers of Learning in 1st grade and stayed with it all the way through she would go through the four year rotation three times, firmly cementing the information in her mind in ever increasing depth. At each level you should expect increasing amounts of outside reading and writing. High schoolers in particular should be reading extensively, and if possible, participating in discussion groups.

These icons will guide you in spotting activities and books that are appropriate for the age of child you are working with. But if you think an activity is too juvenile or too difficult for your kids, adjust accordingly. The icons are not there as rules, just guides.

☺ 1st-4th
☺ 5th-8th
☺ 9th-12th

Within each unit we share:

EXPLORATIONS, activities relating to the topic;
EXPERIMENTS, usually associated with science topics;
EXPEDITIONS, field trips;
EXPLANATIONS, teacher helps or educational philosophies.

In the sidebars we also include Additional Layers, Famous Folks, Fabulous Facts, On the Web, and other extra related topics that can take you off on tangents, exploring the world and your interests with a bit more freedom. The curriculum will always be there to pull you back on track when you're ready.

www.layers-of-learning.com

UNIT FIFTEEN

COLD WAR – U.S. TERRITORIES – CHEMISTRY OF MEDICINE – FREE VERSE

The most improper job of any man, even saints . . . is bossing other men. Not one in a million is fit for it . . .
-J.R.R. Tolkien

LIBRARY LIST

HISTORY

Search for: Cold War, John F. Kennedy, Richard Nixon, Ronald Reagan, Mao Zedong, Nikita Khrushchev, Mikhail Gorbachev, Joe McCarthy, Alger Hiss, CIA, KGB, Berlin Wall, Korean War, Cuban Missile Crisis, Space Race

☺ Cold War Spies by Tim O'Shea.

☺ Spies by Richard Platt. A DK Reader.

☺ Spacebusters: The Race to the Moon by Phillip Wilkinson.

☺ Race Into Space by Eric Arnold.

☺ Sgt. Reckless the War Horse by Melissa Higgins. A picture book that tells the true story of a horse used to carry ammunition during the Korean War.

☺ ☻ Top Secret: Spy Equipment and the Cold War by Sean Stuart Price.

☺ ☻ T-Minus: The Race to the Moon by Jim Ottaviana. Graphic history.

☻ The Cold War by Daniel Turner. Part of the "Simple History" series. The information is not deep, but it covers the major events of the Cold War and helps the student see how things progressed. Lots of images and interesting text.

☻ The Wall: Growing Up Behind the Iron Curtain by Peter Sis. True story of the author's childhood in Prague.

☻ The Berlin Wall by Michael Burgan.

☻ Candy Bombers by Robert Elmer. Mild Christian themes, but not pushy in this historical novel of the early days after the partition of Berlin. First in a series.

☻ The Cuban Missile Crisis by Peter Chrisp.

☻ America in Korean War from KidCaps.

☻ The Soviet War in Afghanistan by Gary Jeffrey. Graphic history, look for other titles in the series.

☻ The Korean War: An Interactive Modern History Adventure by Michael Burgan. We love this series. It allows kids to really get a feel for what it would be like to live in historical times.

☻ ☻ End of the Cold War by Christine Hatt.

☻ The Cold War by Rupert Colley. "History in an Hour" series.

☻ Blacklisted by History by M. Stanton Evans. The story of Joe McCarthy.

☻ Give Me Tomorrow: The Korean War's Greatest Untold Story - The Epic Stand of the Marines of George Company by Patrick K. O'Donnell. Engagingly tells the true story of a brave company of American soldiers in North Korea. Highly recommended, especially for your sons.

GEOGRAPHY	Search for: United States territories, Puerto Rico, Guam, U.S. Virgin Islands, Northern Mariana Islands, American Samoa ☺ Good Night Puerto Rico by Lisa Bolivar Martinez and Matthew Martinez. Picture book about the geography and culture of Puerto Rico. ☻ The Not-Quite States of America: Dispatches from the Territories and Other Far-Flung Outposts of the U.S.A. by Doug Mack. Part travelogue and part political analysis on the culture and importance of the American territories. Entertaining. ☺ Puerto Rico: What Everyone Needs to Know by Jorge Duany. Short history and explanation of politics and culture.
SCIENCE	Search for: medicine, pharmaceuticals, vaccinations. It is very likely that you will find few books at your library on these topics for kids or teens. ☺ ☺ ☻ George's Marvelous Medicine by Roald Dahl. This book is not educational, but it would make a perfectly silly introduction to the chemistry of medicine. In the story George mixes up a big batch of medicine to cure his grumpy grandmother (or poison her). This would make a funny read aloud to spur on discussions for this unit. ☺ ☺ ☻ Medicine News by Phil Gates. This is in newspaper form and features science articles for kids about germs and medicines, focusing on their history. ☺ ☻ Galen and the Gateway to Medicine by Jeanne Bendick. This is the story of Galen, a physician who lived in ancient times. Compare his story to our medicine and medical knowledge of today. ☺ ☻ Louis Pasteur: Founder of Modern Medicine by John Hudson Tiner. This biography is full of fascinating stories and is really well-written. Discusses Pasteur's Christian views. ☻ ☻ Guinea Pig Scientists: Bold Self-Experimenters in Science and Medicine by Mel Boring and Leslie Dendy. Tells the stories of ten scientists who used self-experimentation to learn more about the body and medicine. Should interest kids enormously.
THE ARTS	Search for: free verse, poetry, poetry books for kids, poetry anthologies, poems for two voices. Your library should have a shelf in their children's non-fiction section that is devoted to kids' poetry books; go and peruse it for fun options. ☺ ☺ ☻ Poetry for Young People Series by various authors. Individual poets like Maya Angelou, Langston Hughes, Robert Frost, Emily Dickinson, and many more are featured, one poet per book. ☺ ☺ ☻ Random House Book of Poetry for Children by Jack Prelutsky. ☺ ☺ ☻ Poems To Learn By Heart by Caroline Kennedy. This has lots of great poems for memorizing in a variety of lengths and about all sorts of subjects. ☺ ☺ ☻ The 20th Century Children's Poetry Treasury by Jack Prelutsky. ☺ ☺ ☻ For Laughing Out Loud: Poems To Tickle Your Funny Bone by Jack Prelutsky. ☺ ☺ ☻ Rolling in the Aisles: A Collection of Laugh-Out-Loud Poems by Bruce Lansky. ☺ ☺ ☻ Joyful Noise: Poems for Two Voices by Paul Fleischman. ☺ ☻ Seeds, Bees, Butterflies, and More!: Poems for Two Voices by Carole Gerber.

HISTORY: COLD WAR

Fabulous Fact

The Cold War wasn't really over territory or resources as most wars are. It was fought over control. Would those seeking to govern and control themselves in a free society win, or would those who wanted a small group of elitists to control everybody else win? And which system, communist or capitalist, produces the most wealth and the most well-being?

Fabulous Fact

Nikita Khrushchev visited the United States in 1959, bringing his wife and kids. Disneyland wouldn't let him in, so he visited Sea World instead. Read all about it here: http://www.history.com/this-day-in-history/khrushchev-barred-from-visiting-disneyland

On the Web

Here is a clip of Churchill's Iron Curtain Speech. http://youtu.be/S2PUIQpAEAQ

You can read more of the speech here: http://www.fordham.edu/halsall/mod/churchill-iron.asp

The Cold War was a period of time when the East, led by the Soviet Union, conflicted with the West, led by the United States. The East was communist and totalitarian. The West was capitalist and republican. It was called "cold" because even though the two sides were struggling for power and desired the destruction of one another, they never actually went to war. Though, as we'll see, the fight was fought in smaller theaters around the world.

This is a photograph of the Berlin Wall. The wall separated the people of West Berlin from those of East Berlin in Germany. It was symbolic of the separation between the East and the West during the Cold War. People were free to approach the wall on the West side, so it was covered in graffiti, as you can see in the photograph. On the East side there was a wide strip of gravel watched over by machine gun towers which would shoot to pieces anyone who tried to approach or cross over the wall into free territory. The East side was blank. Photo by Neptuul, CC by SA 3.0, Wikimedia.

The Cold War began with the end of World War II and ended when the Berlin Wall fell in 1989. During World War II, Great Britain, the U.S., and Soviet Russia were allies against the aggression of the Germans and the Japanese. But the only thing that held these allies together was a common enemy. Ideologically, the countries had nothing in common. Communism is the natural enemy of capitalism just as totalitarianism is the natural enemy of freedom. It was inevitable that when "The Big Three," Roosevelt, Churchill, and Stalin, met at Yalta at the end of the war there would be some friction. Stalin got half of Germany and everything east of that line. He also declared war on Japan two weeks before the Japanese surrender so he could claim part of the Pacific as well, ending up with North Korea. The result of World War II was that the world was divided into an East and a West.

In the next decades the war would be fought with bullets in North Korea, Vietnam, Greece, Albania, the Philippines, and Afghanistan. It would be fought with money in Africa, South America, and Asia as less developed nations greedily accepted Soviet money in exchange for becoming Soviet-style dictatorships. It would be fought with propaganda as the Space Race and the Olympic Games "proved" which system produced superior results. And occasionally, it would frighteningly border on an all out war in tense moments like the Cuban Missile Crisis.

The West won the Cold War. It is easy to see that capitalism produces far more wealth and abundance for everyone who is willing to work for it than communism ever could, even under the most enlightened leadership. What's more, communism in the 20th century killed more than 135 million people in peace time according to the U.S. Congressional Record, more than all previous centuries in world history combined. The real number of dead is probably at least four times that many if every death were accounted for.

☺ ☺ ☺ EXPLORATION: Timeline

At the end of this unit you will find printable timeline squares. Cut the squares apart and place them on a wall timeline or in a notebook timeline. They work best when used with the timeline squares from other Layers of Learning units so that you can see what was going on at the same time in different parts of the world.

☺ ☺ EXPLORATION: Communism vs. The American Way

Communism is the idea that money and goods should be taken from the rich and given to the poor to make things fair. To accomplish this, the government must take all property from everyone by force, including bank accounts, investments, homes, farms, factories, automobiles, and stores. Then everyone must be made to accept whatever the government gives them and be satisfied with it. The government owns and controls every aspect of the economy. There is no such thing as private property or profit or working hard to become successful. Communism tries to force equality so that everyone will be equal and happy.

"The American Way" was a catch phase often used during the Cold War in the United States. It meant a set of values that led to

Additional Layer

Even though communism was a failure in every sense, people are still embracing communism. Some of the people who want powerful government to subvert freedom are ignorant, but some are evil. Learning about the Cold War can teach us to spot the evil for what it is, even if it uses different names.

Fabulous Fact

On September 5, 1945, just three days after the end of World War II, Igor Guzinko, a Soviet clerk working in Ottawa, Canada, defected and provided proof of Soviet spy rings in the West whose main job was to steal nuclear secrets. All at once Americans began to fear Russia, who had been an ally during World War II.

Many people mark this as the day that the Cold War began.

On the Web

You can learn more about the CIA spy agency, which was formed during the Cold War, at their website. Play these games: https://www.cia. gov/kids-page/games

Additional Layer

If you were faced with a moral, prosperous, and happy people and you wanted to impose communism on them, where would you start?

In 1958 W. Cleon Skousen, an ex-FBI agent and political theorist, wrote a book called *The Naked Communist*. It outlined 45 goals that the Soviet Communists had in order to subvert and take over America. The 45 communist goals were read into the Congressional Record in 1963 by Congressman Albert S. Herlong Jr, (D) Florida.

If you compare Skousen's list to the *Communist Manifesto* of 1848 and the 1971 *Rules For Radicals* by Saul Alinsky, you'll see some common threads.

Additional Layer

Ask an older person what it was like to do air raid drills and whether he or she was afraid of an atomic bomb.

You might show the person this video too, and ask if he or she remembers watching it as a child: http://youtu.be/IKqXu-5jw60

the freedom, happiness, and prosperity of the American people, as opposed to the way of the East that led to so much suffering, poverty, and death.

Build a set of blocks that show the "American Way." Use this Instructable if you want to build your own blocks from scratch: http://www.instructables.com/id/Build-Blocks/.

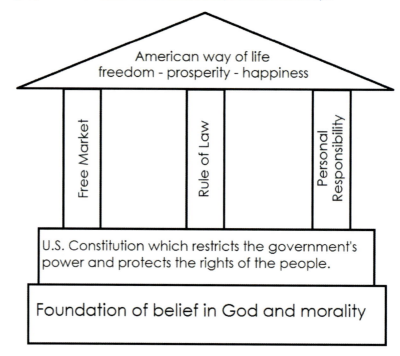

What happens if one of the pillars or the foundation is removed? Does the metaphor hold up in real life? Does the American way begin to disintegrate if people stop respecting the Constitution, for example? What if you're not from the U.S.? Do these principles apply in other countries?

☺ ☻ **EXPLORATION: Berlin Airlift and the Candy Bomber**
Even though the city of Berlin was deep within East German territory, the city had been divided between east and west too. The Soviets tried to cut West Berlin off so they could take the whole city for themselves. Not able to get supplies to the city by road, the West began a huge airlift of food and supplies so the city could hold out against the Russian pressure. This became known as the Berlin Airlift.

People in West Berlin were afraid, hungry, and very alone during this time. One American pilot named Gail Halvorson decided to do something to lift their spirits. He began to drop candy from his plane along with the other supplies. As he flew over the city, little tiny handkerchief parachutes, each with a candy bar or pack of gum dangling from it, would float gently down from his plane.

In the end, over 23 tons of candy were dropped over Berlin, and Lieutenant Halvorsen became known as the Candy Bomber.

Read more about the Berlin Airlift and the Candy Bomber. Then make your own candy parachute. Get a handkerchief, some string, and a package of candy. Create a parachute for your candy. Go up someplace high to drop it off and watch it float down.

☻ ☻ EXPLORATION: Cold War World

At Layers-of-Learning.com you will find a map of the Cold War. It shows which countries in the world were allies of the U.S.S.R. and which were U.S.A.'s allies. There are also spots of conflict shown, places where actual war broke out during these years. Find it here: http://layers-of-learning.com/cold-war-map-world/.

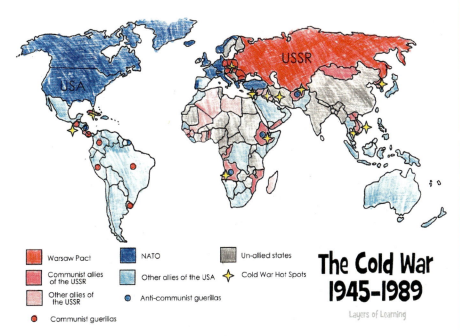

🟥 Warsaw Pact	🟦 NATO	⬜ Un-allied states		
🟥 Communist allies of the USSR	🟦 Other allies of the USA	✦ Cold War Hot Spots		
🟥 Other allies of the USSR	🔵 Anti-communist guerillas			
🔴 Communist guerillas				

The Cold War 1945-1989

Layers of Learning

Additional Layer

Of Stalin, Roosevelt privately said to his adviser, Harry Hopkins:

"I just have a hunch, that Stalin doesn't want anything but security for his country, and I think that if I give him everything I possibly can and ask nothing from him in return, . . . he wouldn't try to annex anything and will work with us for a world of democracy and peace."

This mindset set us up for multiple wars and an ongoing struggle against communist ideas.

Here is more on the Big Three and the conferences: http://www.johndclare.net/cold_war4_personalities.htm

On the Web

Watch "The Responsibilities of American Citizenship," a 1950's film on being a good citizen: http://youtu.be/E1Eld2OqJBM

Fabulous Fact

Notice that China, though it became communist in 1949, did not ally with the U.S.S.R.. China was antagonistic toward nearly everybody during the Cold War but practiced isolationism.

☺ ☺ EXPLORATION: Cuban Missile Crisis

The Cuban Missile Crisis was one of the events of the Cold War between the U.S.A. and the U.S.S.R.. Try a role playing activity to bring to life the Cuban Missile Crisis for kids.

You can find this activity along with a printable set of spy maps and a script for a reader's theater on Layers-of-Learning.com. http://layers-of-learning.com/cuban-missile-crisis-for-kids/

☺ ☺ ☺ EXPLORATION: Spies

The Cold War was the heyday of the spy game. The U.S.S.R. had the KGB, the U.S.A. had the CIA and the FBI, and the Brits had MI5 and MI6.

Some of the techniques real spies used during the Cold War were invisible ink, secret ciphers, dead drops, and recruitment. The Soviets and the Americans were always trying to intercept and decode one another's secret messages, documents, and technology, but most of the information was actually obtained from traitors. Soviet agents at the United Nations and in embassies made friends with and convinced government officials to betray their countries. People would betray their own country for idealism or a fascination with communism, for money, because they were mad at their boss, or because of blackmail. But an agent could never be sure if the person they were propositioning was actually an FBI dangle, someone put there to entrap a spy, or if they were going to squeal. It was a dangerous game.

Play a spy game. Have everyone write their own encrypted secret message on a piece of paper. Hide the papers in plain sight somewhere around the house. The first one to find and decrypt a message wins. There is a top secret spy code instruction sheet at the end of this unit you can print to give your kids some ideas about secret codes and ciphers.

☺ ☺ ☺ EXPLORATION: Communists in America

In 1995, the Venona Project was declassified. Since World War II, the FBI had spent decades collecting data and intercepting Soviet messages without the U.S.S.R. knowing their codes were compromised. The Soviets had a machine that was supposed to generate codes that were unbreakable. But a young cryptologist, Meredith Gardner, broke the code. All of this collecting became known as the Venona Project.

Very, very few people even knew the project existed, including the presidents under whose watch it all took place. The project uncovered the infiltration of spies in the U.S. government to an alarming degree. For example, President Roosevelt's aide, Harry Hopkins, was revealed to be a Soviet agent. Spies were found in the State Department, the Treasury, the Manhattan Project, the upper echelons of the military, and even the Office of Strategic Service (OSS, forerunner of the CIA).

One of the most famously caught spies was Alger Hiss, who was a member of the State Department and part of the establishment of the United Nations, besides advising Roosevelt at the Yalta Conference. Hiss testified before the Senate that he was not a spy and had never been a member of the Communist Party, but later it was found he had lied.

The case of Alger Hiss was extremely controversial at the time. The House Un-American Activities Committee (HUAC) investigated Hiss and thousands of other Americans, including creating a Hollywood blacklist of communists in the film industry. Besides government and film, labor unions and university professors were specifically targeted as communist party members, sympathizers, or spies. Many people saw this as over-the-top hype that was wrecking lives and careers for no reason, while others saw a very real and serious threat.

The revelations of the Venona Project tell us these people really were communist party members, many of them receiving instructions from the KGB. It turns out communists are drawn to certain professions; teaching, entertainment, labor unions, and government are the most common because they are so influential.

But why go after someone merely for their political views? Isn't that un-American all by itself? Don't we believe in freedom of conscience in America?

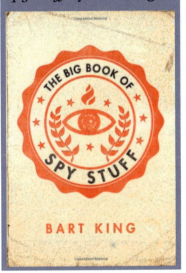

Fabulous Fact

You can read the actual Venona documents at CIA.gov (it's voluminous, but interesting to browse through a bit.)

On the Web

Were the Soviets really infiltrating our government and social institutions to destroy us from within? Yuri Bezmenov, former KGB officer and defector says yes. http://youtu.be/Obr1XqUPEII

Library List

People lost interest in spies when the Cold War ended, but the Soviets are still communists and they're still working to undermine America. The CIA still has its fingers in every pie in the world. An excellent book about post-Cold War spying is *Comrade J: The Untold Secrets of Russia's Master Spy in America After the End of the Cold War* by Pete Earley.

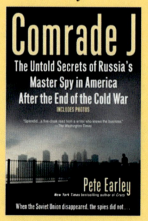

Compare communism to the republican form of American government. If you support communism, does that make you a traitor to your country? Why or why not?

Make a table like the one below to compare the "American Way" to communism and totalitarianism. We've started you out, you can add many more things to the table.

The American Way	Communism
People can choose how to make money and are free to work where and for who they want.	People are forced into certain jobs.
	The government takes care of people's economic needs.
Everyone is subject to the same laws.	

☺ EXPLORATION: The Start of the Korean War

The Korean War lasted from June 1950 until July 1953. It was the first "hot" conflict in the Cold War. But why did the two parts of Korea go to war?

At the end of this unit you will find three different accounts telling how the war started. Compare the three accounts and use the chart, also at the end of this unit, to record how these sources say the war started. Next, look up one or two other sources about the Korean War and read them as well. Write down how you think the war started. Did some sources seem more reliable than others? How did you decide what was true and what was not?

☺ ☺ ☺ EXPLORATION: Battle of Inchon

The North Koreans were far better equipped at the beginning of the war than the South Koreans. The war had been a total surprise to the South. They were quickly pushed back until they held little more than a tip of the peninsula. It took the Americans some time to decide to come to the aid of their little ally and even more time to mobilize from their bases in recently conquered Japan. When they did move, it was under the umbrella of the United Nations and with the aid of fifteen other nations.

U.S. General MacArthur ultimately decided the thing to do was to take the coastal city of Inchon, then move in and take back Seoul, the capital. From there they would relentlessly push the North Koreans across the 38th parallel, the border line that had been decided on after World War II.

The navy shelled Inchon, turning it to rubble. There was little resistance by the time the marines made an amphibious landing. The Americans moved in and, after fierce fighting, took Seoul. Then they stormed across the countryside. The North Korean forces, spread across the South, panicked and tried to flee back to their command in the North. Inchon was a success. The South Korean government was restored, and the Americans had complete control of everything below the 38th parallel by October of 1950.

Watch this three minute video, "Korean War for Kids: U.S. Forces Liberate South Korean Capital from Communist Invaders," on You Tube: https://www.youtube.com/watch?v=5y4h-iHSmOU. It is a newsreel from the 1950s, when this was all happening.

Now use the printable book template from the end of this unit to create a page for each of the countries that fought alongside South Korea. Make four copies of the page so you will have a sheet for each of the sixteen countries. You will have to look up information to finish the blanks on the pages. Staple all the pages together to make one book.

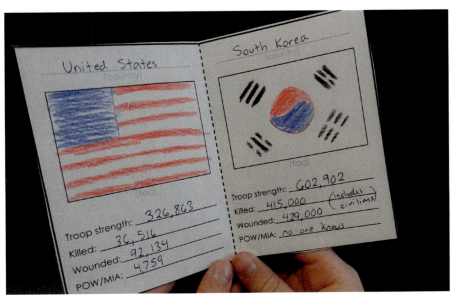

☺ ☻ ☻ **EXPLORATION: The Chinese Join the War**
After the North Koreans were driven out of the South, General MacArthur decided to cross the 38th parallel to really bring North Korea to its knees and force an unconditional surrender. But the Chinese had decided to help the North Koreans if the UN forces decided to cross. So the easy push north that the UN forces expected was met by an enormous force of Chinese soldiers. The UN was forced into a painful retreat, losing many soldiers on the way. The Chinese took back Seoul and the war looked gloomy.

Fabulous Fact

The Soviets never officially joined the war, but they supported the North Koreans and Chinese with money, equipment, and air power. Before going to war in the first place, they had gotten permission from Stalin.

Fabulous Fact

The Korean War was the first in which jet planes fought each other in air-to-air combat. The Russian MiG-15 and the American F-86 Sabre were both used in combat in Korea for the first time.

This is a MiG-15 delivered by a defecting North Korean pilot to the Americans who had offered a reward for it.

Additional Layer

The final result of the Korean War was that just over a million soldiers from both sides were either killed or missing and another 2.5 million civilians were killed. But the borders ended up where they were before the war.

Was anything accomplished by the Korean War at all?

Make a diorama of the UN troops retreating and fighting their way through the bitterly cold winter of 1950 in Korea. Use a box as your base. Add a background with craggy, snow-covered mountains and a gray sky. Use toy soldiers as your figures.

☺ ☺ ☺ **EXPLORATION: Map Timeline of the Korean War**
At the end of this unit you will find a map timeline of the Korean war to print. Each map has a title that tells you which phase it should depict. Find information and a map online or in books on that event and fill in the map on the printable. We have also left circles where you should fill in the dates and a few lines to write a fact or two about the event. Color the maps.

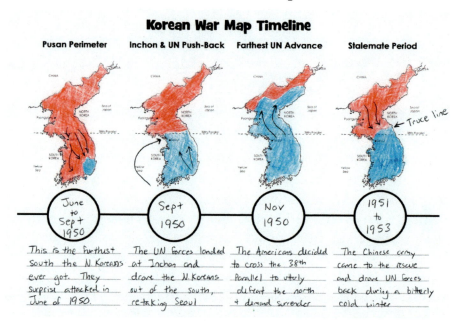

☺ ● EXPLORATION: Space Race

The Space Race was the competition between the United States and Russia to see who could gain control of outer space first. Partly this was just to show who was better, but it was also practical. If you can get a ship into outer space then you can get surveillance equipment and bombs into outer space. What if the Soviets became space capable and put a nuke or other bombs into orbit above the United States? They could launch a debilitating attack with no warning at just the push of a button.

The moment World War II was over the Soviets and Americans were working hard on developing long-range ballistic missiles. Russia and the United States were pretty far away from each other geographically (with the exception of Alaska), and they each wanted to be able to launch destruction at each other from the comfort of their own homes. That led, naturally, to an attempt to get something into space. The Soviets were first with the launch of Sputnik in 1957.

Follow the rest of the Space Race in the Astronaut Training Program printable book at the end of this unit. During the training program kids earn patches upon completion of each stage.

Assemble the book by printing the pages double sided. Fold the pages down the center along the dashed line. Lay the cover face down then the next sheet on top with the Gemini mission on the right hand side. Staple the pages together. After your kids complete the activities they can color in the round mission patch on the lower right side of each page.

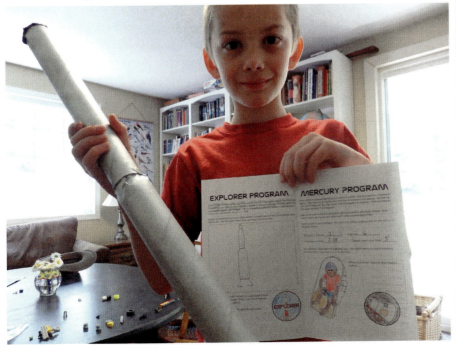

Famous Folks

Wernher von Braun was the premier rocketry scientist working on launching a rocket into space.

Writer's Workshop

Do a biographical sketch of one of the big players from the Cold War era:

Ronald Reagan
Boris Yeltsin
Mikhail Gorbachev
John F. Kennedy
Dwight D. Eisenhower
Joe McCarthy
Richard Nixon

You can use the biographical sketch worksheet from Layers of Learning.

http://www.layers-of-learning.com/character-wanted-posters/

Fabulous Fact

The Vietnam War was a very significant event in the Cold War years. We'll talk about it in detail in Unit 4-16.

GEOGRAPHY: U.S. TERRITORIES

Fabulous Fact

U.S. states are independent "nations," federated together and in equal partnership with the federal government. U.S. territories are owned by the federal government, having no equal relationship.

Fabulous Fact

The legal term "unincorporated" was invented in the late 19th century by the Supreme Court so the U.S. could administer its newly acquired territories any way it liked without having to grant constitutional protections or citizenship.

Fabulous Fact

A commonwealth in U.S. law is an organized, unincorporated territory. It has its own constitution and a right of self-government that cannot be rescinded unilaterally by the U.S. Congress.

Memorization Station

Memorize the five U.S. territories and their locations on a world map.

American Samoa
Guam
Northern Mariana
Puerto Rico
U.S. Virgin Islands

The United States has five inhabited territories including Puerto Rico, Guam, Virgin Islands of the United States, Northern Mariana Islands, and American Samoa. Each of these island territories elects representatives to the House of Representatives of the United States. They have the power to vote in committees, debate on the House floor, and appoint constituents to the United States military academies.

The United States of America

Most of the people who live in U.S. territories are United States citizens. They have protection under the U.S. court system, are guaranteed Constitutional rights and a republican form of government, and pay some taxes (typically social security and Medicaid taxes, but not income taxes) to the U.S. government. They use the United States dollar as their currency and are economically regulated by the United States. They mostly govern themselves locally. The people of Samoa are the only ones who are non-citizen nationals by law. People of the U.S. territories can travel to or live in the United States without visas, and citizens of the United States can live permanently in any of these territories without losing citizenship. These territories are also dependent on the United States military for defense.

Incorporated territories are an integral part of the United States and are fully part of the nation. The inhabitants are U.S. citizens with all the same rights as U.S. citizens everywhere.

Unincorporated territories have fundamental human rights guaranteed to them, but the rest of the Constitution does not apply, unless specified by Congress. Unincorporated territories govern themselves according to their laws and traditions, but with oversight from the U.S. Congress. All of the inhabited U.S. territories are currently unincorporated.

Puerto Rico is the largest of the U.S. territories, in terms of population, with over 3 million inhabitants. Its name is officially the Commonwealth of Puerto Rico, and it is an unincorporated territory of the United States. It is located in the Caribbean Sea, just east of the Dominican Republic and Haiti. In 1898 when the Spanish were defeated by the Americans in war, the islands of Puerto Rico were ceded to the United States. Puerto Ricans were given full U.S. citizenship in 1917. In 1948, they began to govern themselves autonomously, electing their own governor, and adopting their own Constitution in 1952. They are still overseen and legislated by the U.S. Congress, and their president is still the President of the United States, though they do not get to vote in national elections.

The city of San Juan, Puerto Rico.

Guam is located in the Marianas Islands group of the western Pacific and is the largest and most southern of these islands. It has a population of more than 159,000 people. It became part of the United States when it was ceded by the Spanish following the Spanish-American War of 1898. Guam mostly governs itself with local elections, but does not have the level of autonomy that Puerto Rico has.

The Virgin Islands of the United States, commonly called the U.S. Virgin Islands, are located in the Caribbean, just east of Puerto Rico. They have a population of just over 106,000. The islands were sold to the United States by Denmark in 1916. Since 1970 they have elected their own governor. In 2009, they adopt-

Writer's Workshop

Choose one of the territories from the unit, learn more about how it became a U.S. territory, and write a paragraph about it.

Additional Layer

An Organic Act is an official act of the U.S. government that makes a space of land into a territory of the U.S. government, administered by the federal government.

The first Organic Act was the Northwest Ordinance of 1787, which created the Northwest Territory. The most recent was the Guam Organic Act of 1950 which made Guam into an unincorporated territory.

Additional Layer

What makes a country a country?

Read this short article that clearly explains what the criteria is for a country to be considered a country and why Puerto Rico is not one.

http://geography.about.com/od/politicalgeography/a/puertoricoisnot.htm

Famous Folks

Deciding whether to become a state in the United States has been a big deal for Puerto Ricans. In 2012, the people of Puerto Rico voted in a non-binding referendum to determine whether they wanted to change their status as a U.S. territory (51% did want a change of status). If they did want to change, what did they want to become? Of those who wanted a change, 61% voted for statehood. That's still far from a majority of the population, but popularity toward statehood has been growing.

What would be good about admitting a new state from the point of view of America, and what would be bad about it? Does Puerto Rico have a political, economic, and cultural climate that is consistent with the rest of the United States?

Fabulous Fact

Spanish and English are both official languages of Puerto Rico, but very few people actually speak English. In the early 1900s the United States government tried to force the people to change to English. It didn't work.

ed a constitution, but it was rejected by the U.S. Congress in 2010.

The Northern Mariana Islands are in the Pacific, about 2/3 of the way between Hawaii and the Philippines. Their official name is Commonwealth of the Northern Mariana Islands. The islands have a population of over 53,000. The Northern Marianas became a U.S. territory after the U.S. took the islands from the Japanese during World War II. Subsequently, the United Nations gave the territory to the U.S. to administer. In 1975 the Northern Marianas became a commonwealth, with the new government and constitution taking effect in 1978. In spite of Guam being part of the Mariana archipelago and of the same cultural heritage, the two territories have not been politically reunited because Guam harbors ill-feelings following the experiences of World War II (see the Liberation Day Exploration to understand why).

All of the U.S. territories are islands in tropical climates. This is a picture of a beach in American Samoa.

American Samoa is located in the South Pacific, just north of Tonga. It has a population of about 55,500 people. In 1900, the United States declared Samoa to be their territory, with the Germans taking the eastern portion of the archipelago. In 1904, the last sovereign was forced to sign a treaty of cession. The U.S. military governed the islands until after World War II. No Organic Act for Samoa has ever been passed, so it is considered an unorganized territory. In 1978, the military government of the United States ceased, and Samoa elected its first local governor. They govern themselves locally under a constitution, but are administered by the U.S. Department of the Interior. People of Samoa are considered U.S. nationals, but not U.S. citizens. They can travel freely in the United States without a visa, but cannot vote in national elections. They consider themselves self-governing.

☺ ☺ ☺ EXPLORATION: Map of Puerto Rico

Find Puerto Rico on a map or globe of the world. Then color the map of Puerto Rico you will find at the end of this unit.

Next, color the flag of Puerto Rico. The flag traces its roots to the unsuccessful rebellion against the Spanish in 1868, when a flag with the colors and the star was used by rebels. The flag was then outlawed by the Spanish, and later by the Americans, as a symbol and rallying point for rebellion. The flag became the official emblem of Puerto Rico in 1952 when they became a commonwealth of the United States.

The red represents the blood shed by heroes of the rebellion. The white star in the blue field stands for liberty.

☺ ☺ EXPLORATION: Puerto Rican Parrot

Puerto Rico is a beautiful tropical island in the Caribbean. They have gorgeous waterfalls, heavenly beaches, deep teeming forests, and loads of wildlife. One interesting animal is the Puerto Rican Amazon Parrot. It is native to Puerto Rico and can be found nowhere else in the world. It eats fruits, flowers, bark, leaves and nectar all found in the forest canopy. Right now the bird is critically endangered, with only about 80 individuals in the wild.

The parrot is bright green, with brilliant aqua blue on the ends of its wing feathers and a red forehead. Make a parrot of your own out of paper.

Famous Folks

Ricky Martin is a famous pop singer from Puerto Rico who made it big in the United States.

Fabulous Fact

The old San Juan historical district is filled with brightly painted two and three story colonial style buildings. It's filled with shops and cafes, perfect for tourists.

Fabulous Facts

If compared to the United States, Puerto Rico is poorer than the poorest U.S. state, but it is still richer than any other Latin American nation. Its major industries include manufacturing of textiles, pharmaceuticals, and electronics, finance, and tourism.

Find out what is making Puerto Rico suffer economically.

Start with a cylinder of paper for the body and two round circles for the head. The wings and tail are long rectangles of paper cut into strips, leaving the center of the wings in tact and the top end of the tail. The wings should have a double layer of paper with the lower layer a bright blue. Make the beak out of a wide triangle folded in half. Glue all the pieces together and draw on the eyes.

☺ ☺ ☺ **EXPLORATION: Map of Guam**
Color the map of Guam from the end of this unit. Label the Pacific Ocean and the Philippine Sea. Color the flag of Guam.

☺ ☺ ☺ **EXPLORATION: Liberation Day**
During World War II, Guam was attacked and occupied by the Japanese just hours after the attack on Pearl Harbor. For more than two years the people of Guam were tortured, raped, executed, and forced to accept Japanese culture. Many of their masters were actually from the Northern Marianas, which had been a Japanese territory since World War I. On July 21, 1944, U.S. troops

retook the islands. Today this is known as Liberation Day, and it is celebrated each year by the people of Guam. They have parades, floats, military troops marching, bands, dancers, and fireworks.

Read more about the Battle of Guam on Wikipedia. Then watch this video of the Liberation Day festivities and why they celebrate. https://youtu.be/4_eKPYm8pfI.

Design a Liberation Day parade float. You can draw your design on paper or use things like shoe boxes, tissue paper, toilet paper rolls, pipe cleaners, and other craft supplies to create a little model of your float. Include colors and symbols that represent Guam.

☺ ☻ ☻ EXPLORATION: Map of U.S. Virgin Islands
Color the map of the U.S. Virgin Islands from the end of this unit. Find the location of the islands on a map or globe of the world. Notice that on the map we scooted St. Croix north of its actual location so it would fit on the page, but really the islands are further apart. The islands are volcanic and mountainous. They're also tropical with jungles and beautiful white sand beaches.

Color the flag of the Virgin Islands.

This flag was adopted in 1921. It has a simplified U.S. coat of arms and the letters VI for Virgin Islands. The eagle is clutching just three arrows, representing the three major islands. The colors are symbolic too. Blue represents the sea, yellow represents the people, green represents the mountains, white represents the clouds, and red represents love.

☺ ☻ ☻ EXPLORATION: Virgin Islands Dumb Bread
For breakfast in the morning, the people of the Virgin Islands eat

Photo by MARELBU, CC license, Wikimedia.

This man is shelling coconuts for tourists. You can drink right out of them.

either Johnny Cakes (pancakes) or dumb bread. Dumb bread was given that name because it's so easy to make. Try it yourself.

4 cups flour
1 tsp. baking powder
1 tsp. salt
6 Tbsp. butter or shortening

1 Tbsp. sugar
1/2 cup dried shredded coconut
1/2 cup milk

Mix the dry ingredients and cut in the butter or shortening. Add the milk. Knead it for a minute, then shape it into a round loaf and place on a greased baking sheet. Bake at 350 degrees F for 40 minutes.

😊 😊 😊 **EXPLORATION: Map of Northern Mariana Islands**
Color the map of the Northern Mariana Islands, which you will find at the end of this unit. Be sure to look up the location on a world map or globe. Of all these islands, only Rota, Tinian, and Saipan are inhabited. The southern islands are limestone with fringing coral reefs. The northern islands in the archipelago are volcanic. Notice that the deepest oceanic trench in the world, the Mariana Trench, runs parallel with the islands.

Color the flag of the Northern Mariana Islands.

This flag was adopted in 1976. It shows the symbols of the heritage of the islands including a flower lei and a latte stone, a foundation stone in a Chamorro house. The overall design is reminiscent of the United Nations flag since the UN had sovereignty over the territory after World War II.

😊 😊 **EXPLORATION: History Timeline of Northern Mariana**
Research the history of Northern Mariana and make a timeline of the top eight events in the history of the islands. Illustrate the timeline and put it in your geography notebook.

☻ ☻ ☻ **EXPLORATION: Map of American Samoa**

Print the map of American Samoa from the end of this unit. Find American Samoa on a world map or globe. Color the map.

Color the flag of American Samoa.

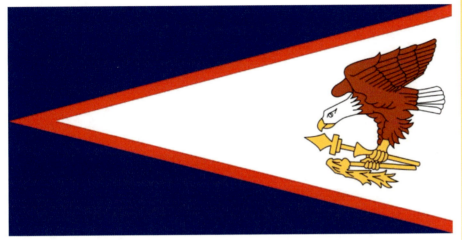

This flag was adopted in 1960 and uses red, white, and blue, the colors of both the United States and Samoa. The bald eagle also represents the United States, but the eagle clutches traditional Samoan symbols, a war club and a fly whisk. The war club represents the power of the government. The fly whisk, a ceremonial mark of authority, represents the wisdom of the chiefs.

☻ ☻ ☻ **EXPLORATION: Three Staples of American Samoa**

American Samoa has a relaxed, laid back lifestyle. No one is in a hurry. You can't go more than 30 miles per hour on any road. There are no big cities, giant corporations, or cubicles. Instead, they have the three staples of their lives: family, faith, and music. Extended families live in neighborhoods next to one another and get together for family events all the time. Nearly everyone in American Samoa is Christian, and there is a lot of social pressure to go to church and pay tithes. They still play their traditional music and dance their traditional dances, but they also listen to American music and make their own island-style rock.

Draw a picture of an island that fills up your page, with water around the very edge. On the island, draw a cluster of houses for the family, a little church for the faith , and then a group of people dancing for the music.

Writer's Workshop

There is an old folk tale that tells the story of how the largest mountains of Tutuila Island in American Samoa came to be. Read the tale, *The Story of Two Brothers*. Draw a picture and write the story in your own words of the mountains of Matafao and Pioa and how the folk tale says they were formed.

http://www.ipacific. com/samoa/brothers. html

On the Web

This woman teaches how to perform a Siva Samoa, a traditional dance. https://www.youtube. com/watch?v=h66ciH-flETg

Fabulous Fact

Per capita, more American Samoans sign up to serve in the armed forces than any other state or territory. This is mostly because they are so patriotic and love their country.

SCIENCE: CHEMISTRY OF MEDICINE

The human body is a chemical-making factory. Your body's systems run based on chemical signals sent from glands, the brain, and substances you ingest or breathe. Doctors can treat illnesses by giving patients chemicals that will interfere with or enhance the chemical signals of the body. They also give medicines to defeat microbes that invade the body.

We tend to think that using drugs to heal illness is a new thing, but it's not. People have been using drugs since at least the time of the ancient Egyptians. Nearly all drugs we use are derived from plants or minerals, even if today we synthesize the plant's drug and take it in pill form. These technicians are making medicine in a lab.

☺ ☻ EXPLORATION: A Rainbow of Medicine

With a parent, go to your medicine cabinet and take a look at all the things that are there. Open the bottles carefully, and look at the pills, syrups, gels, creams, and other medicines. You'll see all kinds of shapes, colors, and sizes. All of these medicines look different, but they are meant to help you feel better when you're sick. They were made by taking substances found in nature that helped people when they were sick, and then changing them into pills, syrups, creams, or other forms. Draw a picture of each of the pills, creams, and other medicines in your medicine cabinet and write the name of the drug and what illness it treats. Talk about why you keep medicines in your house and what it would be like if we didn't have medicines.

☺ ☻ EXPLORATION: Mr. Yuk

While you have all of this medicine out, talk about how taking it when you don't need it, or taking too much, can be harmful. What are some things we should do so that we don't take too much?

Many years ago the Children's Hospital of Pittsburgh created stickers called Mr. Yuk stickers. Dr. Richard Moriarty, a pediatrician, wanted a way for kids to recognize chemicals and medicines they should stay out of. He felt that the skull and crossbones de-

sign that represented poison wasn't right for kids, so he gathered a group of kids together and tested out different designs, asking them which were the ones they would want to stay away from. They chose this face and this shade of green.

You can order Mr. Yuk stickers for free from the children's hospital and put them on your medicine cabinet, cleaning chemicals, or any poisons that could hurt you. They also have the phone number for poison control on them, which you should call if you ever take too much medicine or ingest or come in contact with a harmful poison. The hospital's online store also has coloring books, games, magnets, flash cards, and other tools you can use to teach your kids about harmful substances for purchase. Do an online search for "Pittsburgh Poison Center" for Mr. Yuk resources.

☺ ☺ EXPLORATION: Kinds of Medicines

Medicines work in a few different ways. Often we get sick because germs get in our bodies. Our immune system fights off those germs, but medicines can help our bodies fight them faster or more effectively. Antibiotics are medicines that fight off germs called bacteria.

As our body is fighting off germs we often feel ill, like when we have a fever. A doctor might tell us to take a pain reliever, which doesn't actually heal us, but can make us feel less pain while our body recovers on its own. Cold medicine is another one that doesn't heal us, but helps to relieve our symptoms while our bodies heal on their own. If you rub cream on an itchy bug bite, that cream isn't healing you either. It's just relieving the itch while your body's immune system naturally gets rid of the poison that's causing you to itch.

Another way we get sick is when our bodies aren't making the right amount of a substance we need. For example, people who have diabetes can't make enough insulin, so doctors can give them the insulin their bodies aren't making on their own. Medicines can

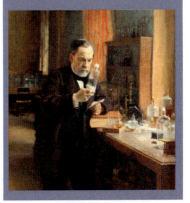

Famous Folks

Alexander Fleming discovered penicillin in 1928, but he wasn't really the one who developed the drug into something that could be mass produced and used medically.

That credit goes to a group of Oxford scientists lead by Dr. Howard Florey, an Australian pharmacologist and pathologist.

Dr. Florey was awarded the Nobel Prize, along with Alexander Fleming and Ernst Boris Chain, in 1945 for the discovery of penicillin.

also block our bodies from making too much of something.

Some medicines actually prevent us from getting sick in the first place. Immunizations are medicines that keep us from catching serious illnesses. When we say we are "getting shots," those are immunizations.

Draw a picture of your body on a notebooking sheet. Show some symptoms, illnesses, and medications. For example, you might show a runny nose, a warm feverish forehead, or a band-aid where you just got an immunization. Around your body, include pictures and captions explaining what medicines are for and what they do.

☺ ☺ ☺ EXPERIMENT: Make Penicillin

Penicillin was the first drug discovered that was effective against bacterial diseases. Penicillin is a mold that stops bacterial cells from producing a cell wall, so when the cell divides it has no cell wall and it dies.

You can grow penicillin at home. You need a lemon, a small canister with a lid, and a little water.

1. Put a lemon with a few drops of water into a tightly closed container.
2. Store it in a warm place for a couple of weeks.
3. Check your lemon to see if it is growing mold. Be careful not to breath in the mold. The penicillin mold is either white or blue-green.

You can take this experiment further and see if your penicillin will inhibit bacterial growth. Coat a nutrient agar petri dish (from a science supplier) with bacteria, from your hands or mouth or skin, applied with a clean cotton swab. Put a bit of penicillin mold near one edge. Put it in a warm place and let it sit for several days. Check to see if you have bacteria colonies growing. Did the bacteria grow where the penicillin mold was growing?

☺ ☺ EXPERIMENT: Resistant Bacteria

Penicillin was discovered in 1928. Since then many other antibiotics have been discovered, but the more we use them, the less useful they become. This is because the antibiotic will kill most, but not all, of the bacteria. The individuals that survive make it because they are not affected as much by the antibiotic. They pass on these resistant traits to the next generation. Pretty soon you have whole strains of bacteria that are resistant to antibiotics.

You can test to see if your bacteria are resistant. You'll

need liquid nutrient agar, antibiotic disks, and petri dishes with solid sterilized agar. You can find all these things from a science supplier like Home Science Tools or Carolina Biological Supply.

1. Prepare some liquid nutrient agar by heating it to nearly boiling for several minutes. Pour it into 3 or 4 clean, sterile, test tubes or small jars (run them through the dishwasher right before you use them) until the test tubes are about ¾ full.
2. Inoculate the agar with bacteria samples. Get one from each person or from different locations in your house. Be sure to label the tubes so you know where they came from later.
3. Put your bacteria in a warm place and let them grow for 4 to 5 days.
4. Sterilize a metal loop (you can unbend a paper clip and use a tightly looped end) by heating it with a flame for several seconds. Let it cool for just a few seconds. Dip the loop into your nutrient agar and then carefully spread it onto solid agar plates, coating the whole surface of your agar.
5. Carefully place antibiotic disks, one of each type you purchased, onto the plates. Label them with the source of your bacteria. Place the plates in a warm place and let them grow for 3 to 4 more days.
6. Observe the bacterial colonies on your nutrient agar. How closely did they grow to the antibiotic disks? The closer they grow, the more resistant they are to the antibiotic.

☺ ☻ EXPLORATION: Drug Receptors

The cells of your body have receptors on their surface. The receptors are there to interact with chemicals your body makes. The chemicals tell the cell to do some job, like divide, or make a protein, or allow some substance to enter the cell, for example. This is how your different systems communicate with each other. But sometimes body systems can malfunction and drugs can be used to interfere with the chemical signals to either block them or facilitate them, depending on what is needed.

This short video shows receptors on a cell and how chemicals interact with them. http://youtu.be/07Tr__R_koE

At the end of this unit you will find a worksheet about the function of the chemical receptors to color.

☺ ☻ EXPLORATION: Antibacterials

Drugs that work to kill or inhibit bacteria do not work on viruses, and the same is true the other way around. Bacteria and viruses are built very differently from one another, and drugs attack spe-

Deep Thoughts

There are arguments for and against isolating the effective properties of a plant and synthesizing it in a lab to make pills or other medications. On the one hand, the dosage can be controlled and side effects reduced when put in pill form. On the other hand, there may be far more going on in the plant's biology than we could ever hope to understand. Are there minor chemicals that make the natural plant a more effective cure?

Additional Layer

Do this experiment with younger kids:

1. Take a swab from unwashed hands and put onto a petri dish with nutrient agar.
2. Rinse hands briefly under water, then take another swab and place on a petri dish.
3. Wash hands thoroughly with soap and warm water, scrubbing under the nails. Then take final swab of your hands and place on yet another petri dish.
4. Label the petri dishes and place in a warm spot for 3-4 days.

Determine together if washing hands makes a difference.

Additional Layer

A lot of the activities in this unit are for older kids. But this is something you can do with all ages.

Ask your kids what they know about bacteria. Write their answers on a sheet of paper. Then look up the answers to these questions together.

- What do bacteria look like?
- How do bacteria move?
- How do bacteria reproduce?
- How are bacteria helpful to humans?
- How do bacteria harm humans?
- Which are harmful bacteria species? What do they do to people?

Make an informational sheet with the answers to each of these questions.

Finish by filling a balloon with hole punch dots. Blow it up and then let the air out at once, showing how the light pieces can spread easily, like bacteria when you cough.

Additional Layer

Vaccines are very controversial in some circles. You should read arguments from both sides and study up on the science before you decide.

cific processes in a living organism.

Likewise, drugs that kill bacteria do not harm the human host. We already learned how penicillin prevents bacteria from creating a cell wall, a process that human cells do not have and therefore cannot be harmed by. Another type of antibiotics are called sulfonamides, sometimes known as sulfa drugs.

Sulfonamides inhibit an enzyme that creates folate in bacteria. Human cells do not make folate at all, we must get it through our diet. So bacteria cells that are denied the ability to make folate won't be killed outright, but they will be weakened, their reproduction rate will be severely reduced, and then your immune system does the rest.

Here is what the sulfa drug chemical structure looks like. The center part, the two oxygens (O), the sulfur (S), and the nitrogen (N), are the core of the sulfonamide. This is what is known as the "functional group." The Rs can be replaced by various chemicals, and that is why you have many drugs that are all sulfonamides.

$$\begin{matrix} O & & O \\ \diagdown\hspace{-0.3em}\diagup & & \diagup\hspace{-0.3em}\diagup \\ & S & \\ R^1 & & N - R^3 \\ & & | \\ & & R^2 \end{matrix}$$

At the end of this unit you will find a printable "How Sulfa Drugs Work" worksheet. Color it and talk about how synthetic or plant chemicals can be made to mimic the shapes of enzymes (body chemicals) and therefore interact with body chemistry.

☻ **EXPLORATION: Synthetic Drugs**
The first person to create synthetic drugs was Paul Ehrlich. Learn more about him, what he did, and why it's so important. Write a one page biography.

☻ ☻ ☻ **EXPLORATION: Vaccines**
Watch this TED ED video called "How do vaccines work?" http://ed.ted.com/lessons/how-do-vaccines-work-kelwalin-dhanasarn-sombut#watch

The four types of vaccines are live attenuated, inactive, antigen, and DNA. Make a poster for each type of vaccine. Include illustrations or printed images. Tell how the vaccines work and which diseases are prevented with this type of vaccine. Here are some common childhood vaccinations: Polio, MMR (measles, mumps, rubella), DTP (diphtheria, tetanus, pertussis), Hepatitis B, and Varicella (chicken pox). Make sure the kids look up the diseases, what their symptoms are, and the death rates from these diseases before vaccines for them became common. Include that information on your posters. Posters from older kids should be much more in depth than posters from young kids.

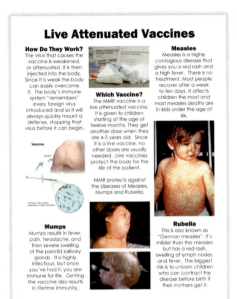

☺ ☺ EXPLORATION: How a Drug is Developed

In the United States, drugs are developed according to rules set up by the federal government. There are several drug companies who hire hundreds of research scientists, mostly chemists and biochemists, to work on isolating chemicals to treat disease. Often the chemicals are from plants, animals, or minerals from the earth.

On the FDA website you can read about how the salmon is being used to treat osteoporosis. http://www.fda.gov/Drugs/DevelopmentApprovalProcess/HowDrugsareDevelopedandApproved/

Then color the worksheet at the end of this unit to see the process a drug has to go through to be prescribed by your doctor.

☺ ☺ EXPLORATION: Aspirin

Salicylic acid, found in willow bark, does the job of killing pain, but it is hard on the stomach. Acetylsalicylic acid does the same job of killing pain, but it is easier on the stomach. In fact, inside your liver your body breaks the acetylsalicylic acid back down into salicylic acid, but notice it has passed through your stomach harmlessly first. Felix Hoffman, a German chemist working for the Bayer company, made acetylsalicylic acid from salicylic acid in 1893. This drug is now known as aspirin.

The synthesis of aspirin is actually really simple. You just mix salicylic acid with acetic anhydride in the presence of a catalyst. Bam! You've got aspirin! Unfortunately, acetic anhydride is also

On the Web

It's been awhile since parents in developed nations have had to worry about their children catching debilitating or deadly childhood diseases. Sometimes we forget how awful these diseases really were. Watch this short video about polio: https://www.youtube.com/watch?v=v-P1Wc-83mY8

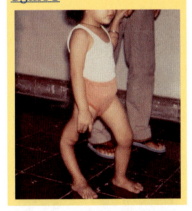

Memorization Station

Enzymes are chemicals in the body that send messages to cells to tell them what to produce or when to divide.

Additional Layer

Talk with your kids about the differences between over-the-counter and prescription medicines.

Talk about correct dosing and only using medicines for the correct symptoms and in the proper way.

You may like this lesson plan from Scholastic: http://www.scholastic.com/browse/article.jsp?id=3757744

Additional Layer

Willow bark is rich in salicylate and has been used as a pain reliever and fever reducer for thousands of years. Learn more about this history.

Additional Layer

Your whole body is a chemical factory with reactions happening constantly and at a rapid rate. The things you eat, the amount of rest and exercise you get, and the vitamins or medicines you ingest all play a factor in how well your chemical factory is working.

Keep a diary for a week or two about the foods you eat and quantities, along with sleep and supplements or medicines. Every day take note of how you feel, both your mood and your health.

used in the synthesis of heroine, and so you can't buy it unless you're a school or a business. Stop doing drugs! You're wrecking my chemistry experiments!

So instead we're going to start with commercial aspirin and decompose it. You need:

- Commercial aspirin tablets
- 70% isopropyl alcohol
- 2 large beakers or glass jars
- Coffee filter
- Funnel
- Salicylic acid (from a science supplier)
- Distilled water

Wear gloves and goggles during this experiment. The acids can be seriously harmful, especially to the eyes!

1. Crush up 15 aspirin tablets. You can use a mortar and pestle (clean please), or put them in a sealed plastic bag and pulverize them with your rolling pin. We're not fussy about your methods.
2. Pour the crushed aspirin into a beaker and use the back of a spoon to crush the bigger bits still left.
3. Aspirin has only two ingredients: acetylsalicylic acid and starch, which is used as a binder. First, we need to get rid of the starch. Do this by dissolving the aspirin in ½ cup of alcohol. Stir.
4. Heat it in the microwave for 30 seconds.
5. Let it sit for 10 minutes. Then line a funnel with a coffee filter. First, fold the coffee filter into quarters then pull back one layer of coffee filter and place, point down, into the funnel. Swirl the solution a bit, then pour the solution through the funnel into a second clean beaker. The white stuff left in your filter is the starch binder. Throw away the filter paper and starch.
6. Next, fill your beaker of solution until it is ¾ full with distilled water. Crystals will begin to precipitate out of solution. Let it sit for one hour or more (it can sit overnight).
7. Line a clean funnel with a clean filter paper as before and pour the solution through, swirling first to get it all in suspension. This time you're saving the white crystals from the filter paper. Lay the filter paper and crystals out on a plate to dry overnight. These are crystals of acetylsalicylic acid.
8. Next, put the white crystals into a clean beaker. You're going to decompose the acetylsalicylic acid into salicylic acid and acetic acid. (You can't get the acetic anhydride because we're doing this in the presence of water, so instead we get acetic

acid). If you just let your crystals sit out in the air they would decompose by themselves over time, but we want it to happen quickly so we're going to use some diluted salicylic acid as a catalyst to get the process moving.

9. Mix 3 ml (½ tsp.) of salicylic acid with 14 ml (3 tsp.) of warm distilled water (preheat the water in the microwave; it should be hot, but not boiling). Pour this over the crystals.

10. Carefully smell your mixture. You should smell vinegar. Acetic acid is the primary component of vinegar that makes it smell and taste the way it does. The sludgy stuff in your beaker is the salicylic acid.

Clean up by washing the chemicals down the sink with plenty of water.

Here is what acetylsalicylic acid looks like:

Do you see that ring of six carbons (the hexagon)? That is the hallmark of an aromatic compound. Aromatic in normal English means smelly, but in chemical terms it just means a compound with a benzene ring (those hexagonal carbons). Some aromatic compounds are quite smelly, but certainly not all. Can you write the chemical formula for aspirin using the diagram? Remember wherever there is a "corner" where two lines join, that indicates a carbon atom, even if it's not written. Also each carbon has four bonds and hydrogen atoms that fill carbon bonds are not usually written either, so don't forget to count the invisible hydrogen atoms.

Here's the answer, but don't peek until you've given it a shot.

$$C_9H_8O_4$$

Additional Layer

Inside the body there are dozens of cycles happening all the time. These are processes that repeat over and over to make your body move, think, use energy, produce vitamins, and so on. Students in medical school study these processes a lot.

When patients are ill, sometimes it isn't because of bacteria or viruses, but because one of these body processes has broken down. If a doctor understands these processes and how they work, she can help the patient get the right diet, lifestyle or medicine changes that help him feel better.

One of these cycles is called the Krebs cycle. This process happens in the mitochondria of every cell. It takes a molecule called pyruvate (CH_3-CO-COO-) and pulls energy from it. Carbon dioxide is made as a by-product of this cycle. It's a pretty complicated series of chemical reactions happening in your body all the time. There are companion processes that regulate how fast the Krebs cycle happens.

Understanding these types of chemical cycles is important for doctors.

THE ARTS: FREE VERSE

Free verse is a modern kind of poetry that is very conversational. It often just sounds like someone is talking to you or just thinking out loud. Free verse poetry doesn't follow the rules of any formulas. It doesn't worry about rhyme schemes or meters or patterns. It doesn't require any specific word play or counting of syllables, or worry over stressed and unstressed words. But although it doesn't require it, these are all still tools a poet can use to create a singsong rhythm, an expectation, a mood, or meaning. Alliteration, onomatopoeia, rhyme, repetition, and other poetry devices can all be used. Free verse poetry is free. The poet can do whatever he or she wishes.

Take a look at this free verse poem called *Growing Garden*. It doesn't rhyme. It doesn't have punctuation. It doesn't obey any rules. Not only does it not capitalize sentences, but it doesn't even have sentences! The only pattern is that the first line in each stanza has 3 words and the second has just one. But the poem ignores syllables. There is no specific format at all. This poem just captures a little moment, a tiny experience. Can you picture the scene? In just 16 words it captures a moment and takes us there. It makes us stop and think about a garden hose, the simplest of things, and in turn, we think about the great impact that even very small things can have.

so much depends

upon

my yellow garden

hose

spraying its life

water

on the tiny

seedlings

During this unit we'll both read and write poems. Some will rhyme and some will not. Some will follow "poetry rules" and others will throw out all conventions. There are no rules required here. Anything goes. Play with and enjoy words. You are even allowed to make up your own words if you wish!

EXPLANATION: Wisdom and Delight
Robert Frost said, "A poem begins in delight and ends in wisdom." That's how I like to think of teaching poetry too. If you want your kids to fall in love with poems, delight them! Begin with silly poems.

> *Adam and Eve and Pinchme*
> *Went down to the river to bathe.*
> *Adam and Eve were drowned -*
> *Who do you think was saved?*

Read lots of lots of silly, fun poetry.

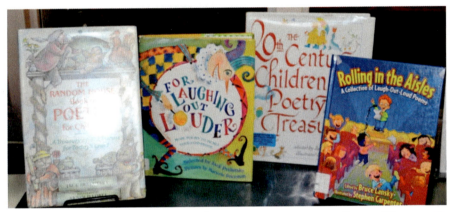

Then, when they are ready, choose some poems that will stretch them and make them think a little, like *Dream Deferred* by Langston Hughes.

> *What happens to a dream deferred?*
>
> *Does it dry up*
> *Like a raisin in the sun?*
>
> *Or fester like a sore -*
> *And then run?*
>
> *Does it stink like rotten meat?*
> *Or crust and sugar over -*
> *Like a syrupy sweet?*
>
> *Maybe it just sags*
> *Like a heavy load.*
>
> *Or does it explode?*

Famous Folks

Ezra Pound had a controversial life. He strongly opposed the World Wars and thought the worst of America. He was a supporter of fascism and of Adolf Hitler, and ended up spending years of his adult life in a mental institution. He wrote many free verse poems, intentionally breaking the rules of writing poems based on syllables.

Memorization Station

Here's a short poem to memorize called "Don't Worry If Your Job Is Small":

Don't worry if your job is small,

And your rewards are few.

Remember that the mighty oak,

Was once a nut like you.

Explanation

If a free verse poem doesn't rhyme and doesn't have to have any special patterns or rhythm, what makes it a poem at all? How is it different than other writing? The truth is, there isn't a clearcut division between poetry and prose. I have read prose that is incredibly poetic. In general though, poetry has more descriptive, decorative language. It relies on imagery. It also doesn't necessarily get arranged into complete sentences and paragraphs like prose. And often poetry isn't grammatically correct.

Additional Layer

Over the history of the world, people have had to memorize all sorts of things. They didn't always have books, pens, and paper, so they memorized stories, recipes, scriptures, and the information they needed for navigating, farming, and trading. In many places there were people within a community whose job is was to remember and share all of the stories and the history of their people. West African griots are an example of this.

The more you read poetry together, the easier it will be for your kids to write poetry. Read more about teaching poetry with wisdom and delight and find some more poetry suggestions here: http://layers-of-learning.com/for-the-love-of-poetry/ .

☺ ☺ ☺ EXPLORATION: My Book of Poems

Make a book of poems that you love. You can copy some silly poems, some of your favorites from this unit, or even write some of your own. Illustrate the book of poems and give your book a title.

Even if you didn't write them yourself, on the cover you can say, "A Book of Poems Collected By _____" and fill in the blank with your name.

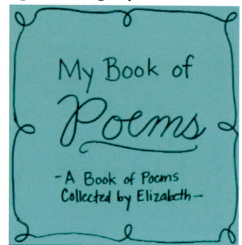

Start by copying this silly poem on to the first page of your book and then illustrating it. For each poem you love during this unit, add it to your Book of Poems.

Way Down South

Way down South where bananas grow,
A grasshopper stepped on an elephant's toe.
The elephant said, with tears in his eyes,
"Pick on somebody your own size!"

☺ ☺ ☺ EXPLORATION: Learning Poems By Heart

The more you memorize, the more you are able to memorize. That seems backwards to some people. It seems like the more you have to remember, the harder it would be, but truthfully, our brains are built to house lots of information. You aren't going to run out of storage space. And the more you learn by heart, the more able your brain is to recall the information. Memorizing is like exercise for your mind. The more you do it, the stronger you become at it. If you aren't used to it, it may feel hard at first, but the more you practice learning things by heart, the easier it will become.

To help you memorize something long, it can help to use a visualization technique called Memory Palace. Picture yourself standing in a big palace. Now imagine objects that represent each idea in the poem and mentally place them in areas as you walk through your palace. Make an effort to really picture the object in its location and remember what it stands for. When it's time to recall the poem, picture walking through that palace, and recall each line as you see its object.

Memorize this poem:

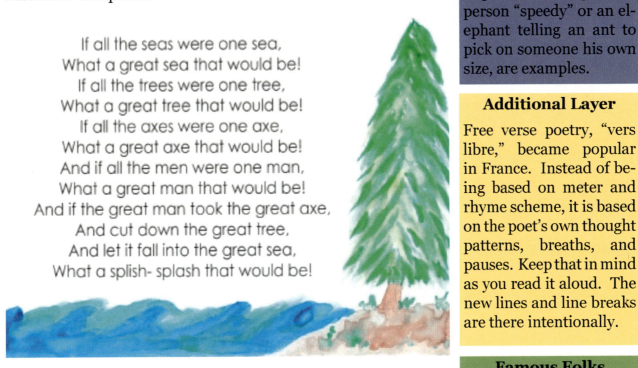

> If all the seas were one sea,
> What a great sea that would be!
> If all the trees were one tree,
> What a great tree that would be!
> If all the axes were one axe,
> What a great axe that would be!
> And if all the men were one man,
> What a great man that would be!
> And if the great man took the great axe,
> And cut down the great tree,
> And let it fall into the great sea,
> What a splish- splash that would be!

☺ ☻ EXPLORATION: Shrink The Sentences

The more I read poetry, the more I am convinced that one of the beautiful gifts of poets is their ability to distill words down to their very most poignant meanings. It's easy to be wordy, but to pack meaning into just a very few words is much harder.

Use these sentences as a guide, but shrink them, keeping only the most impactful words. On the printable from the end of this unit, cross out, rearrange, or change the words of the passage to turn it into a poem. It doesn't need to rhyme or have any special rhythm or pattern. You don't need to worry about complete sentences or grammar. Condense the passage from 200 words to just 50 or less.

I couldn't yet open my eyes. The past 24 hours had been too hard, too full of hurt. My blanket was the only thing that seemed to even be holding me together. From the tips of my toes to every last strand of hair, my whole self ached at the loss of my father. Cancer had stolen him from me like a thief in the night, suddenly and without regard for the searing pain that shot through me at what he took. Eyes closed, I laid there on my bed, dark thoughts and anger and sadness overwhelming me. I was drowning in

Additional Layer

Litotes are understatements. They create irony in poems. Calling a slow person "speedy" or an elephant telling an ant to pick on someone his own size, are examples.

Additional Layer

Free verse poetry, "vers libre," became popular in France. Instead of being based on meter and rhyme scheme, it is based on the poet's own thought patterns, breaths, and pauses. Keep that in mind as you read it aloud. The new lines and line breaks are there intentionally.

Famous Folks

Seneca the Elder, an ancient Roman teacher, had an excellent memory. He could recall and recite 2,000 names in the order he was given them.

Memorization Station

Learn each of these literary devices and try to incorporate them into the poems you write.

Near rhymes are words that almost rhyme. They either share the same vowel or the same consonant sound, but not both.

> Rose
>
> Lose

Assonance involves repeating a vowel sound. It often creates a near rhyme.

> Lake
>
> Fate
>
> Base
>
> Fade

Shakespeare used assonance in this line:

"Shall ever medicine thee to that sweet sleep."

Consonance is similar to alliteration, except that the repeated sound can be anywhere within the words.

> *A rustling salmon sang uncertain songs.*
>
> *He thrusts his fists against the posts.*
>
> *She struck a bad luck streak.*

Enjambment is the continuation of one line of poetry into the next.

*I think that I shall never see
A poem as lovely as a tree.*

---

the darkness in the world and in my heart.

But then, in one moment, it all changed. A bird sang. A tiny glimmer of the beauty of her song coerced my eyes out of their pained squint. And through my window, I saw not only the lovely little bird, but also a light so bright it seemed to penetrate my sadness. The sun, her first morning rays lighting the world, reached her fingers out and brightened every dark place. Light swallowed the darkness. And I knew that even after the darkest of nights, the daylight would come again.

☺ ☺ ☺ EXPLORATION: Memoir Poem

Memoir means "a memory." Choose one of your memories to make into a poem. It might be a vacation or a special holiday memory. Perhaps you remember a big recital, activity, or sporting event you were a part of. Maybe it's the first memory of meeting your new little brother or sister. It might even be a time you were sad or scared. Try to capture the moments of your memory so others can experience what you did. Remember, it doesn't need to rhyme or be in complete sentences. You can begin a new line whenever you feel it's time. There aren't any rules to free verse poetry.

Draw a picture of yourself in the bottom corner of your page, then create a large thought bubble to write the words of your memoir poem in.

☺ ☺ ☺ EXPLORATION: Persona Poem

As we write stories, we often consider the voice we are using. In other words, there is someone in the story who is being the narrator, or telling the story. It is told from someone's point of view. Poets sometimes call their voice the poem's "persona." Who is the person speaking? Does the poem's word choice and tone change depending on who is behind it?

Here is a little poem called *Mom's Gone.* It is clearly from the point of view of a child who misses Mom very much.

There's a waking up in the morning
Where Mom ought to be.
There's a combing my hair and getting dressed
Where Mom ought to be.
There's a breakfast, lunch, and dinner
Where Mom ought to be
There's a going to dance class
Where Mom ought to be.
There's a story time
Where Mom ought to be,
There's a tucking into bed
Where Mom ought to be.

Additional Layer

A refrain is a repeating line within a poem. In *Mom's Gone*, the refrain is the line, "Where Mom ought to be."

Refrains can create a rhythmic sound without requiring any creative rhyming. They can also assert an important point in a poem through repetition.

How would the poem be different if it were about the same situation, but from a different point of view? The poem doesn't specify whether Mom passed away, is missing, if she is too sick to be there, if she's on vacation for a bit, or whether she just left for good because she wanted to, but clearly she is gone. Choose one of those scenarios and a character within it. Perhaps Mom is so sick that she's in the hospital. Tell the story from the point of view of the doctor who is treating her. Or perhaps Mom died. Tell the story from the point of view of Dad, who also misses her and is watching his children and doesn't know how to help them. Or maybe Mom is on vacation because after years and years of housework and kids, she needed a week to find herself again. You could tell that one from the point of view of Mom herself.

Whichever persona you choose, write a poem from that point of view and think about how that changes not just what is said, but how it is said. Will you use the same repeating line? Will the lines be short like these, or longer and more lyrical? Will it be full of hurt or full of hope?

😊 😊 😊 EXPLORATION: Poetry For Two Voices

A poem for two voices is like a conversation. It is written for two people to perform out loud. It is usually written in columns - one for each person reading the poem, and sometimes a third column that both readers speak in unison.

Watch this performance of several poems for two voices called *Two Voice Poetry* by katiematheison2 on YouTube: https://youtu.be/DaCYcDbol9o.

Use the Poetry For Two Voices printable to read and then write some two voice poems.

Famous Folks

John Greenleaf Whittier was an American Quaker poet. Many of his poems were made into hymns. He became famous for his poems that spoke out against slavery in early America. After the 13th amendment to the Constitution formally ended slavery, he began writing poems about other things, his cause finally won. He was also a big supporter of women writers.

Memorization Station

What is a stanza? A stanza is a bit like a poet's version of a paragraph. In free verse poetry, stanzas can be any length and any number of lines. You could have a one line stanza or a one hundred line stanza if you chose.

No matter what kind of poem you're writing, stanzas of certain lengths have names. Memorize them:

couplet: 2 line stanza

tercet: 3 line stanza

quatrain: 4 line stanza

Additional Layer

Figurative language is another name for imagery. Personification, simile, metaphor, and allusion are all kinds of figurative language, where we compare one figure with another thing or idea.

You don't have to compare people with animals all the time. You could compare the evening sunrise to a red rubber ball falling. You could compare a fish's scales to old, brown peeling wallpaper. Or you could say that the quilt was brightest sunshine. Try some that don't involve animals.

☺ ☺ ☺ EXPLORATION: Imagery

Something that sets poems apart from other writing is imagery. Imagery is visually descriptive language. It helps us picture something in our minds, often by using something familiar to us to represent something else. Here are some examples of imagery:

He fell down like an old tree in a windstorm.

The surface of the lake was like glass.

Autumn had arrived; the fiery tree was ablaze with color.

Imagery tries to link something familiar to something unknown. Perhaps I have a friend, but you don't know her. I want to describe her to you so that you can picture the kind of person she is, even though you've never met her. I could tell you all sorts of things about her, or I could use imagery to help you "see" who she is in your mind's eye. I'll start by writing my friend's name and then I'll list 3 characteristics about how she is on the outside (her appearance), and 3 characteristics about how she is on the inside (her personality). I look only at the adjectives on each row, and decide on an animal that has those characteristics.

Lyla is . . . tiny, delicate, young (a butterfly)
. . . strong-minded, courageous, determined (a lion)

Then I eliminate the adjectives and make the comparison.

Lyla is a butterfly, but her heart is a lion.

That's imagery. Hopefully, without me saying much more, you can picture the kind of person she is.

Try it. Think of someone you know. Write down his or her name. Describe 3 appearance adjectives and 3 personality adjectives. Decide on animals that share those adjectives, then create the imagery.

Now describe other things using imagery. You don't have to use people and animals. Compare the thing you're describing to something familiar and tell about it vividly. Write 10 sentences that each use imagery.

☺ ☺ ☺ EXPLORATION: Upside Down Poem

Free verse poetry lets you be completely creative with how you arrange your words. You can group your lines and stanzas any way you like. You can also make your words climb up the page or fall down the page.

Or you can write an upside down poem like this one:

Everything looks different
when I'm standing on my head.

Shoes and knees
As far as I can see.

The doors are flying way up high;
The chimneys touch the ground.

The sun shines below my feet,
And the sky is grass green.

You try it. Think of a situation that would cause you to be upside down and write a little upside down poem about it.

☺ ☺ ☺ EXPLORATION: Doodle Poem

A doodle poem lets words and pictures work together. It works best if it's some kind of story and scene that involves action. Let your words participate in the action as you write and doodle your poem. Take a look at this doodle poem, and then write one of your own.

☺ ☺ ☺ EXPLORATION: Sights, Smells, and Sounds

When we write poetry we often speak of sensory language, or descriptions that are based on our senses of sight, smell, or sound. Imagine that you were going to pack up some sights, smells, or sounds in a bag to take them along with you.

On the Web

Famous children's poet, Kenn Nesbitt, has some great tips for kids about writing free verse poetry on his website.

https://www.poetry-4kids.com/news/how-to-write-a-free-verse-poem/

Writer's Workshop

T.S. Eliot, who wrote many famous free verse poems, said, "No verse is free for the man who wants to do a good job."

What do you think he meant? Write about what you think it takes to write a good free verse poem.

Teaching Tip

Family photos are a great resource if kids are having trouble with getting inspiration to write a poem. Photos have a powerful way of bringing back vivid memories. The photo of my daughters on this page was taken in their grandma's flower garden while they were helping her. Imagine all of the sights, sounds, smells, and emotions that this one picture holds for them. Pull out a family photo album to get ideas.

I'm going on a trip today,
But I can't bear to leave them.

Into my magic bag they'll go
My favorite smells, I'll take some.

The grass, fresh clipped
The rosebuds, just opening
My dog, wagging hello
The muffins from the oven
Popcorn, dripping with butter
Pine trees, deep in woods
Oranges, just peeled

What sights, smells, or sounds would you take along? Choose one of the senses - sight, smell, or sound. Write a poem about what you would take in your magic bag.

☺ ☺ ☺ **EXPLORATION: One Word Stands Out**

In free verse poetry, one fun technique poets use is putting just one word on a line. If there is only one word on a line, that word can't help but be noticed. It is usually an important word or idea, important enough to stand all by itself.

Rain rushing down,
Engulfing me,
Soaking me,
Worries wash away.
Lightning flashes,
Nature's fireworks.
Thunder rumbles,

Grounding my troubles.
Peace
In a storm.

The word "peace" stands all alone on its line. Think about how different the whole poem would be if that one word said "Fear" instead of "Peace." The one word gave the poem direction. It shaped what it was about. Write one of your own.

😊 😊 😊 EXPLORATION: Your Very Own Free Verse

Decide on a theme you'd like to write about. It can be anything that you would like to express on paper. As you think about that thing, what words come to mind? Write them all down. Brainstorm as many words or phrases as you can about your topic.

Look over your brainstormed ideas and think about ways you can create imagery. Make some comparisons or decide on some vivid language that will help others see your topic the way you do.

Remember to consider your senses, especially the sights, smells, and sounds you can incorporate. If you want to, you can also add in some word play, rhymes or near rhymes, alliteration, or other figurative language.

Now it's time to write your poem. It doesn't need to have any special format and it doesn't need to rhyme, so you should be able to incorporate most of your ideas into your poem. Once you've written it, make sure to add it to your Book of Poems if you're keeping one.

Teaching Tip

When you're learning to write poetry, writing a whole poem can feel overwhelming. Do lots of word play and figurative language practice before you write the poem. It's like loading your toolbox with the tools you need before starting to build.

Allusions are easy techniques to practice. An allusion is a reference to something or someone famous.

This snippet of a poem from *Snowbound* by John Greenleaf Whittier alludes to Aladdin:

"*A tunnel walled and overlaid With dazzling crystal: we had read*

Of rare Aladdin's wondrous cave,

And to our own his name we gave."

Coming up next . . .

Unit 4-16

Vietnam War
Atlantic States
Food Chains
Photography

My ideas for this unit:

Title: _____ **Topic:** _____

_____
_____
_____
_____
_____
_____
_____
_____
_____
_____

Title: _____ **Topic:** _____

_____
_____
_____
_____
_____
_____
_____
_____
_____
_____
_____
_____
_____

Title: _____ **Topic:** _____

_____
_____
_____
_____
_____
_____
_____
_____
_____
_____
_____
_____
_____

Title: _____ **Topic:** _____

_____
_____
_____
_____
_____
_____
_____
_____
_____
_____

Title: _____ **Topic:** _____

_____
_____
_____
_____
_____
_____
_____
_____
_____
_____
_____
_____

Title: _____ **Topic:** _____

_____
_____
_____
_____
_____
_____
_____
_____
_____
_____
_____

Korean War

This is an Australian soldier comforting Korean kids after their village has been cleared of enemy soldiers. The children had been hiding, and the soldier told them it was safe to come out.

The Korea War was part of the Cold War. Communist China and Russia wanted Korea to become communist and the United States wanted it to be free. The two sides had decided to divide up Korea, but the North Koreans wanted the country united. American, Australian, New Zealander and other troops all fought for freedom in Korea alongside South Korean troops.

Cold War Timeline

Feb 8, 1945	**March 5, 1946**	**June 1948**	**April 1949**
Conference at Yalta divides the East from the West	In a speech Churchill describes an iron curtain descending across Europe	Soviet blockade prompts the Berlin Airlift	NATO founded to resist Communist aggression. Warsaw Pact formed in the east.

June 1949	**August 1949**	**April 1950**	**June 1950**
"Red Scare" reaches its peak when American celebrities are named as communists	U.S.S.R. successfully tests a nuclear bomb	U.S.A. declares a foreign policy of communist containment	North Korea invades South Korea, beginning the Korean War

October 1957	**April 1961**	**August 1961**	**October 1962**
Sputnik successfully launched	Bay of Pigs invasion of Cuba ends in disaster	Berlin Wall is built by the Soviets	Cuban Missile Crisis
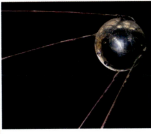			

July 1969	**Feb 1980**	**June 1987**	**Nov 1989**
First man lands on the moon	U.S. Hockey team beats the Soviets at the Lake Placid Winter Olympics	Reagan demands "Mr. Gorbachev, tear down this wall!"	Revolutions across Eastern Europe begin to break out; the Berlin Wall is torn down after peaceful protests

Top Secret Codes and Ciphers

These are top secret codes used by our super secret spy agency. Do not let the enemies get their hands on them.

CLASSIFIED

A1Z26 Code
Substitute numbers for letters.

A	B	C	D	E	F	G	H	I	J	K	L	M	N	O	P	Q	R	S	T	U	V	W	X	Y	Z
1	2	3	4	5	6	7	8	9	10	11	12	13	14	15	16	17	18	19	20	21	22	23	24	25	26

ASCII Code
A computer code that substitutes numbers for letters thus:

A	B	C	D	E	F	G	H	I	J	K	L	M	N	O	P	Q	R	S	T	U	V	W	X	Y	Z
65	66	67	68	69	70	71	72	73	74	75	76	77	78	79	80	81	82	83	84	85	86	87	88	89	90

ATBASH Code
This is just the alphabet substituted for the alphabet written backwards.

A	B	C	D	E	F	G	H	I	J	K	L	M	N	O	P	Q	R	S	T	U	V	W	X	Y	Z
Z	Y	X	W	V	U	T	S	R	Q	P	O	N	M	L	K	J	I	H	G	F	E	D	C	B	A

Code Words
Substitute entire phrases for words. The person receiving the code must have the key, a code book with all the phrases you might use.

Accountant	Come at once.
Alligator	Meet me tonight.
Banana	Abort mission.
Boston	Someone is watching.
Orange	Give the papers to your contact.
Street	Enemy agent.

Caesar Cipher
Shift the letters forward 3 or any other number.

A	B	C	D	E	F	G	H	I	J	K	L	M	N	O	P	Q	R	S	T	U	V	W	X	Y	Z
X	Y	Z	A	B	C	D	E	F	G	H	I	J	K	L	M	N	O	P	Q	R	S	T	U	V	W

Spelling Errors
Write a natural sounding letter to your contact, but put in spelling errors. Every mistaken letter forms the real message.

Hi Amy! Can you meet me for lunch? Does Wednesday at noon worc for you? I am hoplng your Auntie May con come alongs as well, so ask her, wen't you? See you soon as possitle! -Michelle

Words In Skip Code
Every third word is the real message.
Swat the y. It is for my brother. Your shoe kills life.

Different Points of View on the Korean War

	How did the Korean War start?
North Korean Textbook	
South Korean Textbook	
British Textbook	
How I think it all started	

Korean War Accounts

North Korea Textbook

History of the Revolution of our Great Leader Kim Il-sung: High School. Pyongyang: Textbook Publishing Co., 1999, 125-27.

…The American invaders prepared for war and invasion in 1950, the 39th year of the Juche calendar. The American imperialist called the traitor Sungman Lee to Japan and gave him the order to hurry the war, while frequently sending warmongers to the South in order to survey the preparation of the war…

The American invaders who had been preparing the war for a long time, alongside the puppets, finally initiated the war on June 25th of the 39th year of the Juche calendar. That dawn, the enemies unexpectedly attacked the North half of the Republic, and the war clouds hung over the once peaceful country, accompanied by the echoing roar of cannons.

Having passed the 38th parallel, the enemies crawled deeper and deeper into the North half of the Republic. A grave menace drew near our country and our people. His Excellency, the great leader of the Republic, had a crucial decision to make- the invading forces of the enemies had to be eliminated and the threatened fate of our country and our people had to be saved…

South Korea Textbook

Kim, Doojin. Korean History: Senior High. Seoul: Dae Han Textbook Co., 2001, 199.

When the overthrow of the South Korean government through social confusion became too difficult, the North Korean communists switched to a stick-and-carrot strategy: seeming to offer peaceful negations between the leaders of the South and the North aiming toward a constitution of a unified government, and openly publicized their policy. By that time the American forces stationed in the South withdrew and announced that the peninsula would be excluded in America's first line of defense in the Far East. Taking advantage of this situation, the North Korean communists prepared themselves for war. Kim Il-sung secretly visited the Soviet Union and was promised the alliance of the Soviets and China in case of war. Finally, at dawn on June 25th, 1950, the North began their southward aggression along the 38th parallel. Taken by surprise by these unexpected attacks, the army of the Republic of Korea (South Korea) fought courageously to defend the liberty of the country. But with the lack of soldiers and equipment, Seoul had to surrender and the South Korean forces were forced to retreat to a battle line south of the Nak-dong River. The armed provocation of the North Korean communists brought the UN Security Council around the table. A decree denounced the North Korean military action as illegal and as a threat to peace, and a decision was made to help the South. The UN army constituted of the armies of 16 countries- among them the United States, Great Britain and France- joined the South Korean forces in the battle against the North.

Great Britain Textbook

Sauvain, Philip. The Modern World: 1914-1980. Cheltenham: Stanley Thomas, 1989, 314-18.

When Japan was defeated in 1945 the Allies were faced with the problem of deciding the future of the old Japanese empire. The Korean peninsula had been Japanese since 1910. The Allies (but not Stalin) promised it would become independent after the War. But in 1945 it was partitioned along the 38th parallel with the Japanese forces surrendering to the Red Army in the north and to the Americans in the south.

Plans to unite the two halves failed, so in 1948 both occupation zones were granted their independence. The Republic of Korea (formerly the American zone in the South), led by Syngman Rhee, came into being on 15 August 1948. The Korean People's Democratic Republic (formerly the Soviet zone in the North), led by Kim Il Sung, was founded on 9 September. The Soviet forces left North Korea by the end of 1948. US forces left South Korea by June the following year.

Neither of the two Korean governments was happy with the partition of their country. Both claimed to be the rightful government. The United Nations tried in vain to unify the two Koreas as both sides built up their armed forces. Not surprisingly, there were frequent skirmishes on the frontier between the two Koreas. In 1949, the UN commission in Korea warned of the danger of civil war.

An uncomfortable peace kept the two sides apart until 4am, Sunday 25 June 1950. A large North Korean army led by Marshal Choe Yong Gun, supported by tanks, crossed the border and rapidly moved south. Its seven divisions easily outnumbered the four poorly equipped South Korean divisions which faced them.

_____
(country)

(flag)

Troop strength: _____

Killed: _____

Wounded:_____

POW/MIA: _____

_____
(country)

(flag)

Troop strength: _____

Killed: _____

Wounded:_____

POW/MIA: _____

_____
(country)

(flag)

Troop strength: _____

Killed: _____

Wounded:_____

POW/MIA: _____

_____
(country)

(flag)

Troop strength: _____

Killed: _____

Wounded:_____

POW/MIA: _____

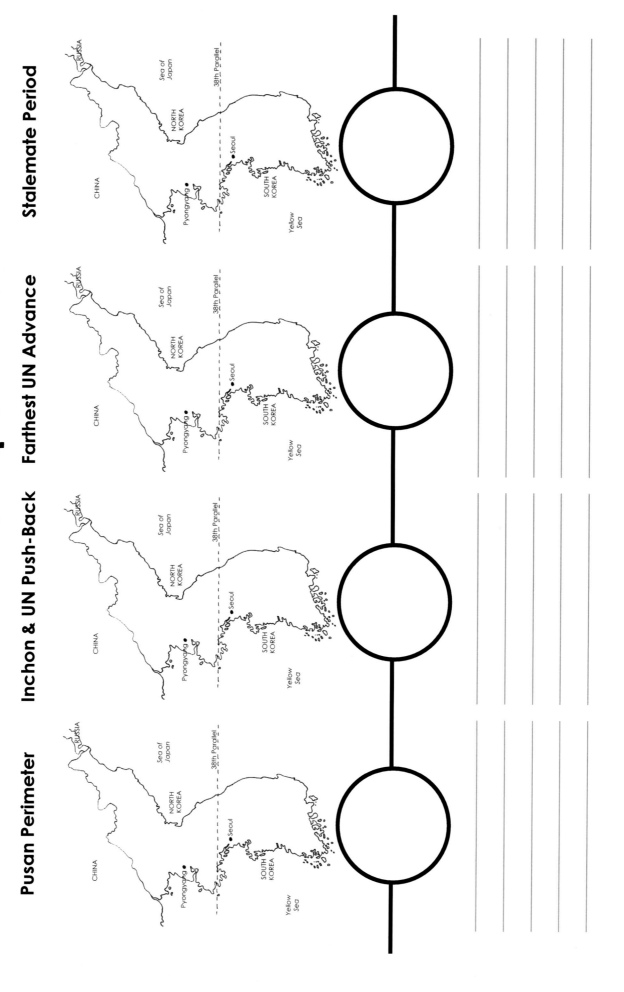

Korean War Map Timeline

Pusan Perimeter

Inchon & UN Push-Back

Farthest UN Advance

Stalemate Period

SPACE RACE
Astronaut Training Program

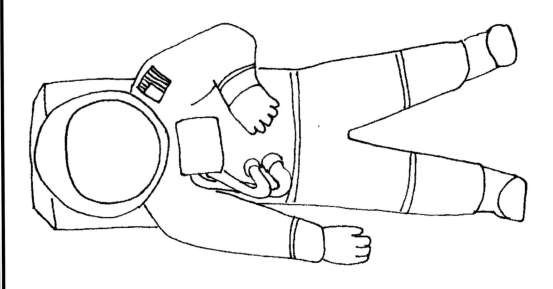

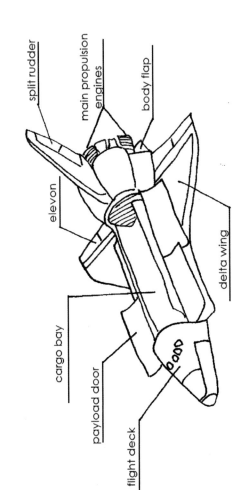

split rudder

main propulsion engines

body flap

elevon

delta wing

cargo bay

payload door

flight deck

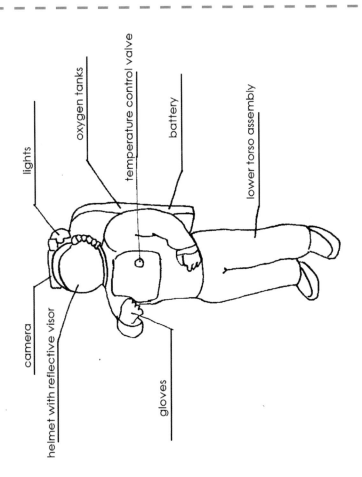

lights

oxygen tanks

temperature control valve

battery

lower torso assembly

camera

helmet with reflective visor

gloves

SPACE SHUTTLE

The Space Shuttle was designed to have the main aircraft be reusable. The boosters, filled with fuel, can only be used once though. The Space Shuttle could also carry large payloads into space in the center compartment. The Hubble Space Telescope and the International Space Station were both carried into space using the Space Shuttle. The Shuttle takes off like a rocket, but lands on a runway like an airplane.

Label the parts of the shuttle from the word bank below. The answers are on the back cover of this book.

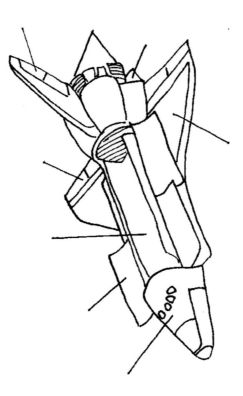

flight deck	payload door	cargo bay	delta wing
elevon	split rudder	main propulsion engines	body flap

After you label the Shuttle parts, find a video of a Shuttle launch on the internet. Watch it.

Color the mission patch when you are finished.

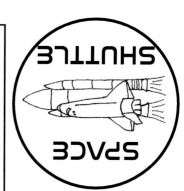

EXPLORER PROGRAM

After the Soviets launched Sputnik successfully, the Americans began the Explorer Program to get their own rocket into space. Werner von Braun and his team did calculations and built models. The first American rocket in space was Explorer 1, which was launched January 1, 1958.

Design a rocket of your own. Remember, rockets have to be symmetrical and balanced. Tail fins keep them from spinning out of control.

After you design your rocket you can build it from stuff around the house. When you have finished, color in the mission patch.

EXTRA CREDIT: Buy, build, and launch a real model rocket.

MERCURY PROGRAM

After NASA mastered getting a rocket into orbit, they focused on manned flights. The Mercury Program put the first American into space. His name was Alan Shepard. But he wasn't the first person in space. That had been a Russian named Yuri Gagarin.

Men who went into space had to be in excellent physical condition. They were mostly Air Force test pilots with science backgrounds.

See if you're in good shape. Record your times and counts on the chart of physical fitness.

Sit-ups in one minute _____   Push-ups in one minute _____

1/4 mile (400 m) run time: _____   Reach past your toes: _____

Test animals were sent into space too. The most famous was a monkey named Ham. You can color his picture.

When you finish, color in the mission patch.

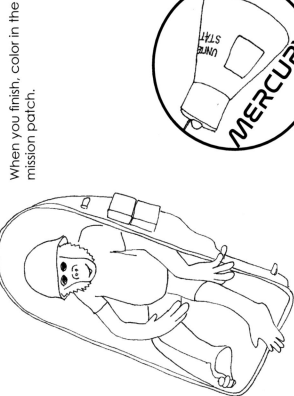

SKYLAB MISSION

Skylab was the first permanent space station. On Skylab, science experiments were done. Skylab was converted from a stage 3 Saturn V rocket. It was launched into space in one piece.

One of the science experiments done on Skylab was to grow crystals in zero gravity. You can grow crystals at home.

1. Make a saturated solution of salt in water. Heat 1/2 cup water and stir in salt, 1 spoonful at a time until no more salt will dissolve.
2. Pour the salt solution onto a piece of sponge and allow the water to evaporate for several days.
3. Draw a picture of your salt crystals in the box.

Go online and find a picture of crystals grown in zero gravity. Are they different from your crystals?

When you finish, color in your completed mission patch.

APOLLO PROGRAM

The Apollo Program had the goal of putting humans on the moon. Early Apollo missions orbited the moon, and then, in 1969, Buzz Aldrin and Neil Armstrong landed on the moon in Apollo 11. Michael Collins orbited the moon in the space craft while the other two collected samples and did some experiments. Five more later Apollo missions landed on the moon as well. The Apollo Program is one of the greatest achievements of mankind.

Look at the labeled moon below. You can see the six Apollo landing sites labeled with the number of their mission. Go outside on the night of a full moon and see if you can spot the locations of these sites and some of the major landmarks of the moon.

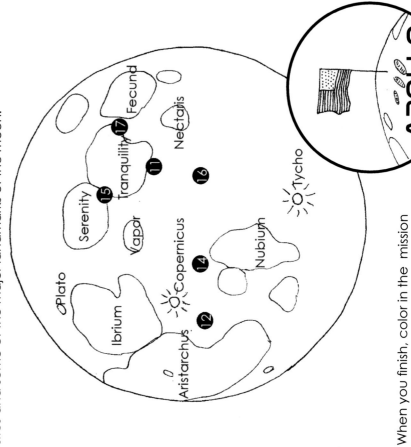

When you finish, color in the mission patch.

GEMINI PROGRAM

The Gemini Program was designed to help NASA learn enough to put men on the moon. They learned to dock two space craft together, to do science experiments while in space, to be in space for at least nine days, and to do space walks outside the space craft.

Label the diagram of the space suit using the word bank. Answers are on the back cover of this book.

lower torso assembly

camera   lights

gloves   battery

temperature control valve

oxygen tanks

helmet with reflective visor

Build your own space suit with things from around your house. Try hammering in a nail or typing on a keyboard with your space suit on.

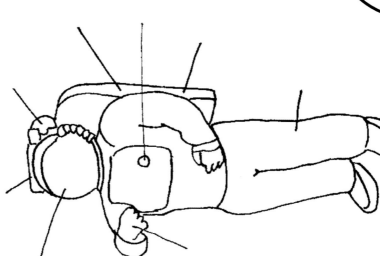

Color in the mission patch when you finish.

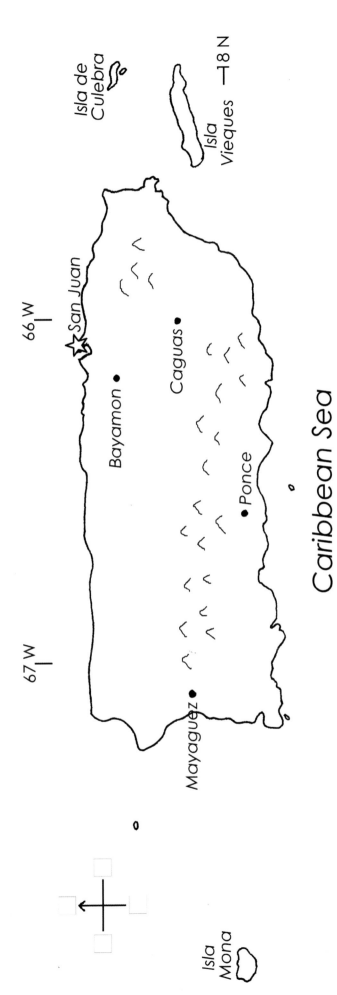

Isla de
Culebra

Isla
Vieques ─┤8 N

San Juan

66 W

Bayamon ●

Caguas ●

67 W

● Ponce

Mayaguez ●

Caribbean Sea

Isla
Mona

Puerto Rico

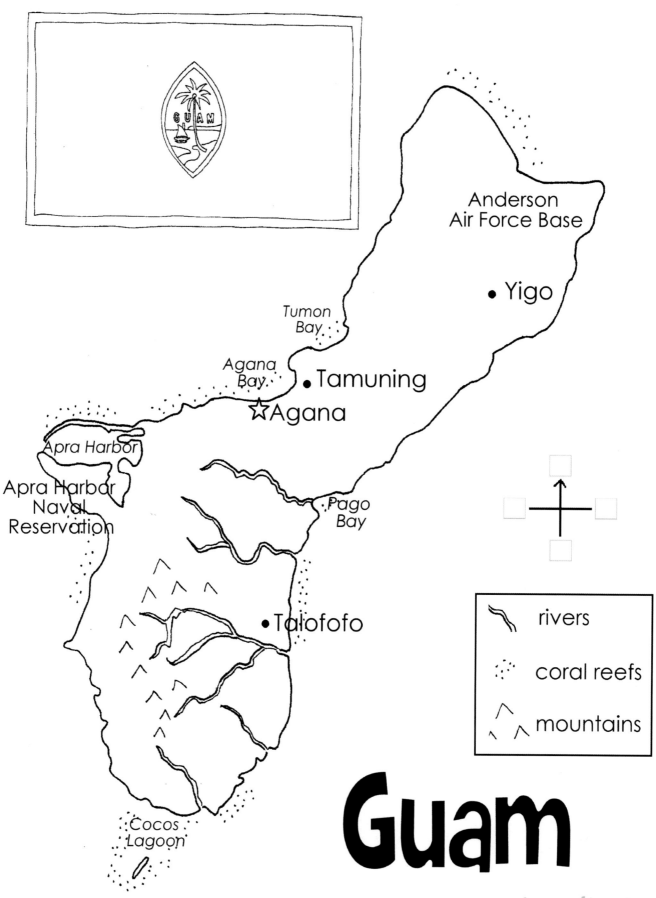

Anderson
Air Force Base

• Yigo

*Tumon
Bay*

*Agana
Bay*   • Tamuning

☆ Agana

Apra Harbor

Apra Harbor
Naval
Reservation

*Pago
Bay*

• Talofofo

rivers

coral reefs

mountains

*Cocos
Lagoon*

Guam

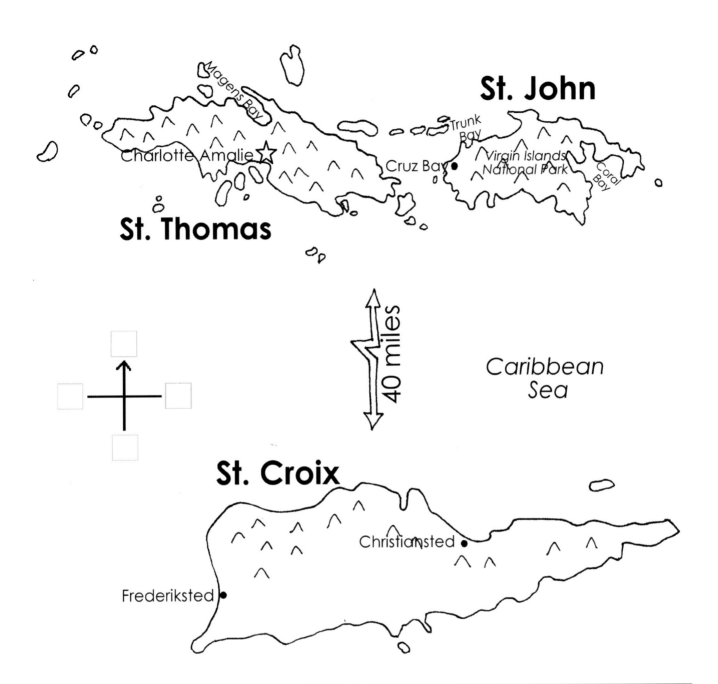

St. John

Magens Bay

Charlotte Amalie

Trunk Bay

Virgin Islands National Park

Cruz Bay

Coral Bay

St. Thomas

40 miles

Caribbean Sea

St. Croix

Christiansted

Frederiksted

U.S. Virgin Islands

V I

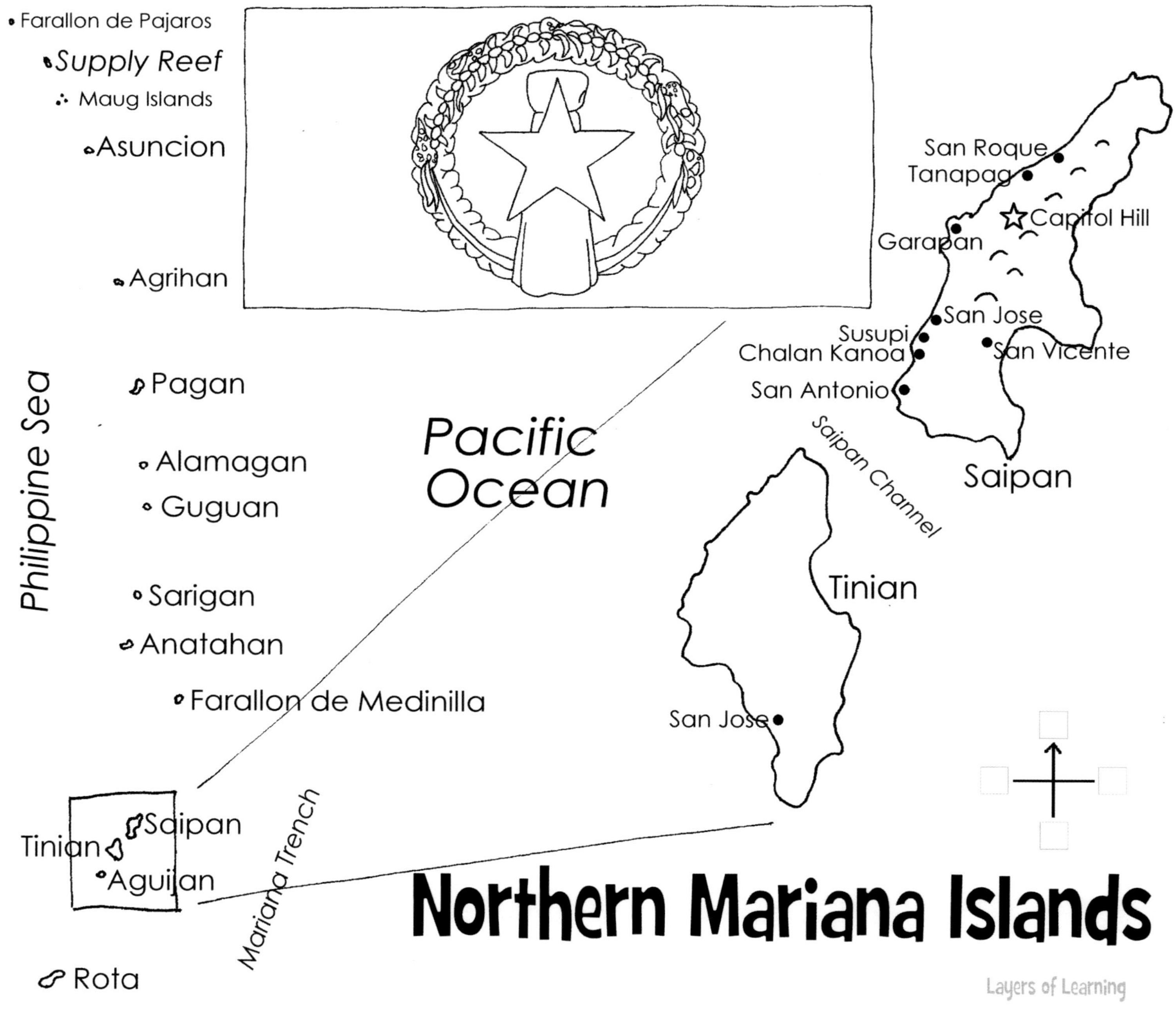

Northern Mariana Islands

Capitol Hill

San Roque
Tanapag
Garapan
San Jose
San Vicente
Susupi
Chalan Kanoa
San Antonio

Saipan

Saipan Channel

Tinian

San Jose

Pacific
Ocean

Philippine Sea

Farallon de Pajaros

Supply Reef

Maug Islands

Asuncion

Agrihan

Pagan

Alamagan
Guguan

Sarigan
Anatahan

Farallon de Medinilla

Tinian
Saipan
Aguijan

Mariana Trench

Rota

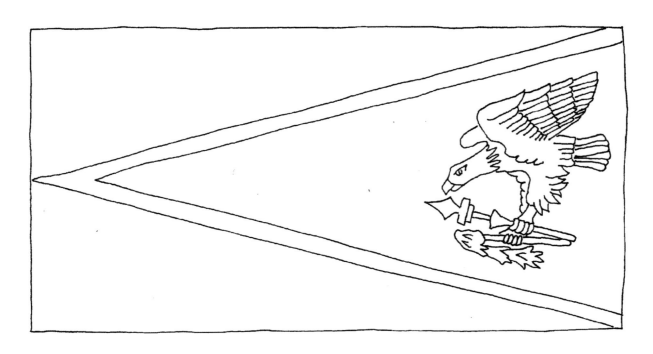

Olosega
Ofu °° ♡
Ta'u

Tutuila

Rose Atoll

Pacific Ocean

Pola
Island

Vatia

Tutuila

National Park
of Samoa

Tula

Pago Pago ☆

Aua

Fagatogo •

Utulei

Aunu'u
Island

• Aasu

• Poloa

Tafuna •

Leona •

• Vaitogi

American Samoa

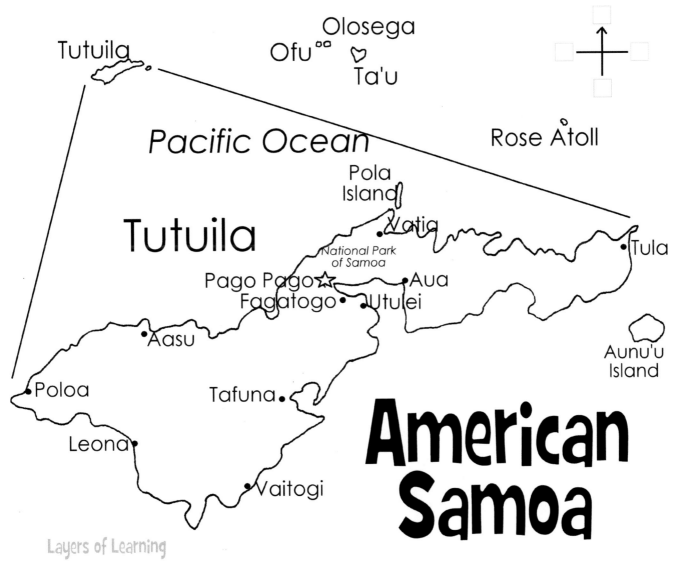

Chemical Receptors and Drugs

Color the diagram of the cell receptors and the effect drugs have
on chemical signals that the body sends

Here the drug is aiding the body in sending more of
the desired signals to the cell.

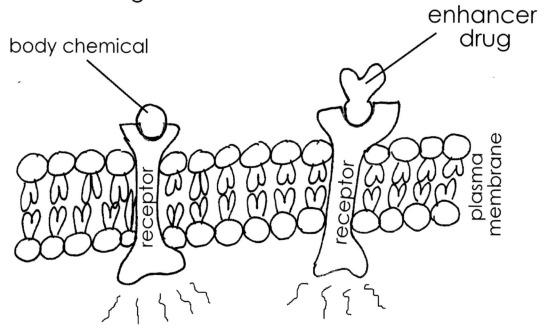

Here the drug is blocking the receptors and stopping
the body from sending undesired signals.

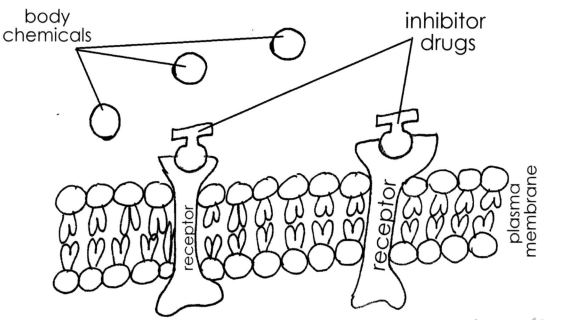

Antibaterial drugs work by blocking specific bacterial cell processes. This diagam shows a sulfa drug blocking the receptors that would normally recieve signals from enzymes telling the bacteria cell to produce folate. The drug enters human cells too, but human cells do not produce folate so no human systems are disturbed.

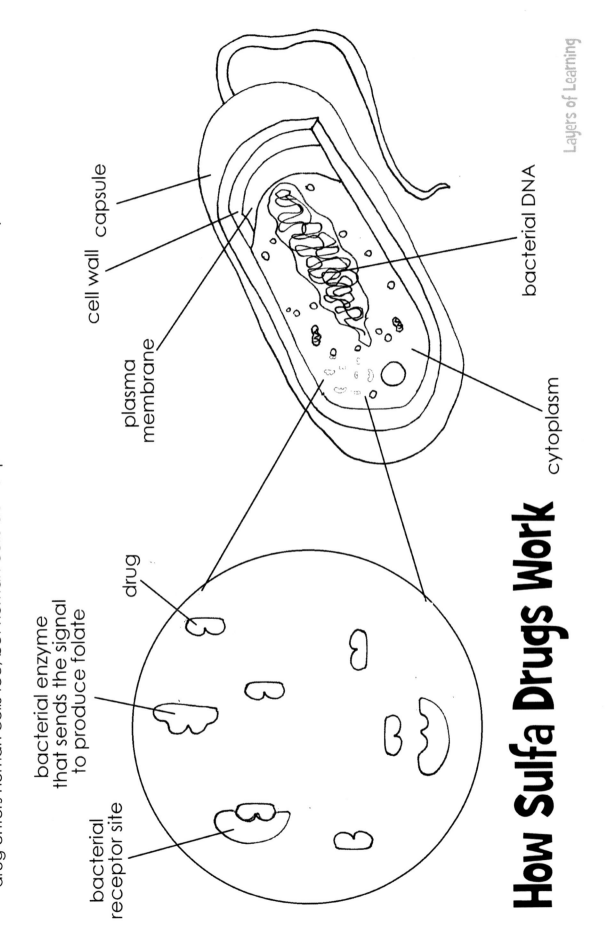

cell wall   capsule

bacterial DNA

plasma
membrane

cytoplasm

drug

bacterial enzyme
that sends the signal
to produce folate

bacterial
receptor site

How Sulfa Drugs Work

How a Drug is Developed

Osteoporosis is a disease that breaks down hard bone structure and makes it very easy to break a bone. It happens because cells in the body called osteoclasts break down bone tissue. Osteoclasts are supposed to be regulated and inhibited by calcitonin, but some people as they age don't produce enough. But it turns out that salmon produce calcitonin too and theirs works even better than human calcitonin.

Biochemists in a lab learn how to make synthetic calcitonin like the salmon's.

Salmon produce potent calcitonin

Once they have their data, the drug company submits an Investivational New Drug application to the FDA.

Once the IND is approved the drug company does clinical trials on humans who have osteoporosis.

After the clinical trials are finished the drug company submits a New Drug Application. Once that is approved, the drug goes on the market.

Shrink The Sentences

Use this sheet to condense, rearrange, replace, and cross out words from this passage to turn it into a poem that is 50 words or less. It doesn't need to rhyme or have complete sentences. Write your finished poem at the bottom of the page.

I couldn't yet open my eyes. The past 24 hours had been too hard, too full of hurt. My blanket was the only thing that seemed to even be holding me together. From the tips of my toes to every last strand of hair, my whole self ached at the loss of my father. Cancer had stolen him from me like a thief in the night, suddenly and without regard for the searing pain that shot through me at what he took. Eyes closed, I laid there on my bed, dark thoughts and anger and sadness overwhelming me. I was drowning in the darkness in the world and in my heart.

But then, in one moment, it all changed. A bird sang. A tiny glimmer of the beauty of her song coerced my eyes out of their pained squint. And through my window, I saw not only the lovely little bird, but also a light so bright it seemed to penetrate my sadness. The sun, her first morning rays lighting the world, reached her fingers out and brightened every dark place. Light swallowed the darkness. And I knew that even after the darkest of nights, the daylight would come again.

_____

_____

_____

_____

_____

_____

Poetry For Two Voices

Read this poem for 2 voices. The first reader will read the Voice #1 column. The second reader will read the Voice #2 column. Both readers will read in unison in the Both Voices column. Make sure to pay attention to line placement so you know when it's your turn to read. Once you've read the first poem, write your own poem for two voices.

Voice #1	Both Voices	Voice #2
I am Batman.		I am the Joker.
I am a hero.		I am a villain.
I fight crime.	We are enemies.	I am crime.
People admire me.		People fear me.
Without the Joker		Without Batman
	I am nothing.	

Voice #1	Both Voices	Voice #2

About the Authors

Karen & Michelle . . .
Mothers, sisters, teachers, women who are passionate
about educating kids.
We are dedicated to lifelong learning.

Karen, a mother of four, who has homeschooled her kids for more than eight years with her husband, Bob, has a bachelor's degree in child development with an emphasis in education. She lives in Idaho, gardens, teaches piano, and plays an excruciating number of board games with her kids. Karen is our resident arts expert and English guru {most necessary as Michelle regularly and carelessly mangles the English language and occasionally steps over the bounds of polite society}.

Michelle and her husband, Cameron, have homeschooled their six boys for more than a decade. Michelle earned a bachelors in biology, making her the resident science expert, though she is mocked by her friends for being the Botanist with the Black Thumb of Death. She also is the go-to for history and government. She believes in staying up late, hot chocolate, and a no whining policy. We both pitch in on geography, in case you were wondering.

Visit our constantly updated blog for tons of free ideas,
free printables, and more cool stuff for sale:
www.Layers-of-Learning.com

Made in the USA
Middletown, DE
04 April 2025

73769536R00040